The Silver Archive #1C

SAPPHIRE & STEEL

Assignments Five and Six

By James Cooray Smith

THE SILVER ARCHIVE

SAPPHIRE AND STEEL - ASSIGNMENTS FIVE AND SIX

ISBN: 9781909031784

Published by Obverse Books, Edinburgh

Range Editor: Stuart Douglas

Cover Design: Cody Schell

First edition: August 2018

10 9 8 7 6 5 4 3 2 1

Text © 2018 James Cooray Smith

A CIP catalogue record for this title is available from the British Library.

2018 Titles

The Silver Archive #1a: **Sapphire & Steel** *Assignments 1 & 2*

    - David and Lesley McIntee

The Silver Archive #1b: **Sapphire & Steel** *Assignments 3 & 4*

    - Cody Schell

The Silver Archive #1c: **Sapphire & Steel** *Assignments 5 & 6*

    - James Cooray Smith

The Silver Archive #02: **Stranger Things**: *Season 1*

    - Paul Driscoll

The Silver Archive #03: **The Strange World of Gurney Slade**

    - Andrew Hickey

The Silver Archive #04: **Buffy the Vampire Slayer**: *Innocence*

    - Jon Arnold

CONTENTS

OVERVIEW — Assignment Five

Serial Title: Assignment One
Writers: Don Houghton (1, 3,4) and Anthony Read (2, 5, 6)
Director: Shaun O'Riordan

Original UK Transmission Dates:	11 August 1981
	12 August 1981
	18 August 1981
	19 August 1981
	25 August 1981
	26 August 1981
Running Times:	Episode 1: 25m 00s
	Episode 2: 23m 40s
	Episode 3: 23m 10s
	Episode 4: 24m 40s
	Episode 5: 25m 00s
	Episode 6: 25m 00s
UK Viewing Figures:	Episode 1: 16%
	Episode 2: 19%
	Episode 3: 17%
	Episode 4: 21%
	Episode 5: 17%
	Episode 6: 18%

[As percentage of the viewing audience]

Regular cast: Joanna Lumley (Sapphire), David McCallum (Steel)

Guest Cast: Patience Collier (Emma Mullrine), Davy Kaye (Lord Mullrine), Nan Munro (Felicity McDee), Jeremy Child (Howard McDee), Jeffery Wickham (Felix Harborough), Jenny Stoller (Annabelle Harborough), Peter Laird (Greville), Stephen Macdonald (Dr. George McDee), Christopher Bramwell (Tony Purnell), Patricia Shakesby (Anne Shaw), Debbie Farrington (Veronica Blamey), Valentine Dyall (Radio cricket commentator)

Antagonists: Time/It, viral bacteria, and Emma Mullrine.

Critical Responses:

'It could afford to lose an episode or two and it's not the creepiest, but I like its ideas and its Agatha Christie aesthetic. I also think guest writers was just what the series needed. It's not a typical **Sapphire & Steel** story, if only for the sheer size of its cast, but I like that too.'

[Finn Clark, *Sapphire & Steel Assignment 5*, April 2010]

'What might have been a clever twist on country-house murder mysteries or J.B. Priestley's *An Inspector Calls* is frittered away on an unconvincing resolution that reduces Sapphire and Steel to mere spectators.'

[John Coulthart, *Haunted Corridors: The Temporal Enigmas Of Sapphire And Steel*, March 2015]

OVERVIEW — Assignment Six

Writer: P.J. Hammond

Director: David Foster

Original UK Transmission Dates:	19 August 1982
	24 August 1982
	26 August 1982
	31 August 1982
Running Times:	Episode 1: 24m 20s
	Episode 2: 24m 00s
	Episode 3: 24m 20s
	Episode 4: 24m 20s
UK Viewing Figures:	Episode 1: 16%
	Episode 2: 16%
	Episode 3: 15%
	Episode 4: 15%

[As percentage of the viewing audience]

Regular cast: Joanna Lumley (Sapphire), David McCallum (Steel), David Collings (Silver)

Guest Cast: Edward de Souza (Man), Johana Kirby (Woman), Christopher Fairbank (Johnny Jack), John Boswall (Old Man)

Antagonists: The Transient Beings.

Critical Responses:

'Not a lot makes sense, but then very little ever did in this show. It's all brilliantly acted by the central trio and it is such a shame that this was the last outing that they ever had.'

[SciFiFreakSite.com, Assignment 6]

'A terrific character-led piece of drama [which] ends in a wonderfully evocative and unsettling manner that would be far beyond the scope of a lesser TV show.'

[Dave Duntun, 'Story Reviews', *Sapphire & Steel Omnibus*]

Introduction

Any piece of writing about **Sapphire & Steel** will almost certainly be reduced to invoking certain adjectives before it's through, with the series inevitably being described as enigmatic, ambiguous, mysterious, inexplicable and/or opaque. This superfluity of adjectives is, of course, exactly because the series is not terribly easy to describe. Its two protagonists, their relationships to each other, the nature of their work, for whom they work and why, the extent of their powers and abilities, and even whether they are human, are, somehow, only a few of the things about the programme which are purposefully ambiguous.

'Ambiguous'. There's another one.

This not-quite-comprehensible aspect of the series' content is – in a way that cannot be deliberate and which is as frustrating as it appropriate – extended to the circumstances of its writing, production and even transmission. The incomplete and inaccessible nature of the Associated Television paperwork archive means that **Sapphire & Steel** is a series the production of which it is not easy to write about with any certainty.

We cannot be absolutely sure even when the fifth serial, the first of the two covered in this volume, was produced, only that it must have been complete before it was shown (time paradoxes and confusions of cause and effect like those its script deals with being the stuff of fiction). For anything more specific we are reliant, again not inappropriately given the nature of the programme, on the fallible human memories of people involved.

The third, fourth and fifth **Sapphire & Steel** serials[1] formed a second production block of the series. This was commissioned at some point in 1980 and followed the successful broadcast of the second serial (which formed the final eight parts of an initial production order of fourteen) after the conclusion of the 1979 ITV strike[2].

The three new serials were, it seems, both written and produced very quickly, so much so that series' writer/creator PJ Hammond, who had written every episode of the first four serials, found himself simply unable to proceed with writing a fifth.

'I didn't write the fifth story, because I was still writing against the clock, and I'd probably written too much in a short space of time; I was quite exhausted by that time and I couldn't think of something within the time[scale] available. So, Shaun [O'Riordan, producer] had to find somebody else to fill that gap.'[3]

With a month to go until immovable studio dates, and with Hammond's blessing, Anthony Read[4] was approached, not by

---

[1] As named in these volumes *Assignments Three* to *Five*, although these descriptions are no more 'authentic' than the fan derived, and somewhat lurid, titles applied by the Internet Movie Database or terming the serials *Adventures* rather than *Assignments* as the nineties VHS releases of the series did. Hammond later decided the second serial would have been called The Girls That Gave Them Flowers (*Counting Out Time* — 14m) had a title been asked for.

[2] A once notorious, now largely forgotten, industrial dispute which saw Britain's then only commercial station replaced by an apologetic test card for two months.

[3] *Counting Out Time* — 22m 40s

[4] Anthony Read (1935-2017) was a writer, producer and story editor, whose contributions to **Doctor Who** are probably the most remembered examples of a long career in television which included series such as **Z Cars**

O'Riordan but by the series Executive Producer (and ATV Head of Drama) David Reid who was working with the writer on other projects. Anthony Read was enthusiastic, but busy himself with his work as Story Editor of **Hammer House of Horror**. He accepted the assignment but suggested that he split the writing of the serial with Don Houghton. The two were not close friends, but they shared an agent (which simplified contractual matters) and as a one of the then-owners of Hammer, Houghton was arguably in some sense Read's boss.

There was, unusually, no bible for **Sapphire & Steel**, explaining the characters and concepts[5]. While this was in part because no one had anticipated anyone other than Hammond authoring episodes, it is likely the oblique nature of the series played its part in the lack of ready explanations. The writers then, were left to create their own version of Sapphire and Steel, based on their impressions of the programme as it had already been made and transmitted.

Sitting together at Read's home for a day, the two writers worked out a story between them, and divided the serial's six episodes evenly when it came to the actual scripting[6]. Houghton would write Parts 1, 3 and 4, and Read Parts 2, 5 and 6. The most obvious influence on Read and Houghton's serial, and one which Read acknowledged after the fact, is Agatha Christie's *And Then There*

(1962), **The Troubleshooters** (1965-9), **Chocky** (1984) and its sequels and *The Baker Street Boys* (1985) for which he won a Writers Guild of Great Britain Award.

[5] Callaghan, Richard, *Assigned: The Unofficial and Unauthorised Guide To Sapphire And Steel* (Ebook 62%)

[6] The episodes credit them individually, with neither receiving acknowledgment for their storylining on the other's episode, nor credit for material reused from earlier episodes, e.g. the repeat of Houghton's final scene for Episode One as the cold open of Read's Episode Two.

Were None (1939)[7]. Interestingly, this is a book which has been one of star Joanna Lumley's favourite novels since childhood[8], although the **Sapphire & Steel** serial derived from it is her declared least favourite of the six[9].

One of the most celebrated of the then very recently dead Dame Agatha's novels, *And Then There Were None*, itself adapted many times for stage and cinema, sees ten characters picked off, one by one, after they arrive on an island and are then cut off from the mainland and all outside contact. The resemblance, with the Mullrine family and their guests being trapped inside the house by a break in time, and being picked off similarly, is little more than superficial. That said, aspects of the book are occasionally invoked in dialogue in the serial, most noticeably in Felicity McDee's statements 'And then there were eight!' (and variations thereupon) after certain murders are committed. It has also been noted[10] that a phrase from the novel 'Two judges, who didn't come from this world at all' could be seen as the inspiration for inserting Sapphire and Steel themselves into a version of this story for television.

That 'for television' is important. It may seem odd, after three decades of ITV's **Poirot** and in the midst of another Christie revival, this time at BBC One, that in the late 1970s Agatha Christie's works were not merely not the television staple they are now, but that they were specifically barred from being made due to Dame Agatha's own dislike of the medium. The first significant television production of any Agatha Christie novel, *Why Didn't They Ask Evans?* had been transmitted on 30 March 1980, a very short time

---

[7] Previously published under a different title
[8] Lumley, Joanna, *No Room for Secrets* (2004)
[9] *Counting Out Time,* 23m 11s
[10] *Assigned* 62%

before Read and Houghton were engaged to work on **Sapphire & Steel**. With high viewing figures, strong critical response and, crucially, the strong approval of the Christie Estate, it was seen as one of ITV's biggest recent successes.

A spiritual sequel, an adaptation of *The Seven Dials Mystery*, would be made and broadcast before *Assignment Five* managed to be transmitted, and would become one of the ten most watched television programmes of 1981. *Assignment Five*, then, is a very specific intervention in a then emerging television trend. The early twenty first century equivalent would be to pitch the characters without warning into a pastiche of a Scandinavian television drama or 'Nordic Noir'.

This engagement with contemporary television trends is not the only way that *Assignment Five* sticks out among its P.J. Hammond scripted brethren. Not only does it have the largest cast of any **Sapphire & Steel** serial, it has a larger cast than the other five serials put together. What's more, everyone in the serial, except Sapphire and Steel themselves, is a real flesh and blood human being. Unlike in the other assignments, there are no ghostly plague victims or Roundheads or Tommies, no suddenly dangerous transformed objects or faceless men. Thus, while the story itself is, with its literary antecedents and greater reliance on humour than the rest of the series, unusually arch, it is also the most concerned with human beings, their emotions and their relationships with one another – and to an extent that perhaps effects the characterisation of the series' leads.

Once completed, the scripts were accepted by producer/director O'Riordan and rushed into production. Anthony Read's personal archive indicated that the serial was written in the weeks

15

immediately before an August 1980 recording[11]. (It is likely the script for this serial, simply by virtue of it not being by Hammond, that O'Riordan would later recall 'working through the night'[12] in his ATV office with McCallum in order to 'fix'.) Actress Patricia Shakesby, who played Lord Mullrine's secretary Anne Shaw in the modern-day sections of the serial, recalled that the programme was recorded set by set 'as you do when you do a big movie'[13], rather than weekly and in narrative order, and as some earlier **Sapphire & Steel** serials seem to have been[14], and that the recording was prefaced by a complete read through of all six episodes attended by the entire cast[15].

Ironically, after all this frantic activity, the transmission of the serial was delayed for almost exactly a year, with Episode One debuting on ITV on 11 August 1981. It is interesting to wonder if any of the original audience noticed temporal discontinuities unrelated to plot that resulted from this delay. The story takes place in 1980, with 1930 repeatedly said to be 'fifty years ago', with the term used

---

[11] *Assigned* 59%

[12] *Counting Out Time* 17m

[13] *Assigned* 60%

[14] Shaun O'Riordan recalled that **Sapphire & Steel** would have been impossible to shoot as 'a straight through show' i.e. more or less 'as live' as some ATV productions were made even in the late 1970s, (Commentary on *Assignment One*, Episode One, 21m) but that does not preclude the programme being made on an episode by episode basis and/or in story order, it merely means that the production made use of recording breaks when needed. It is also possible that the Anne Shaw scenes are a special case in that the character only appears on one set. Even an otherwise story order recording might choose to shoot all the scenes on a single set featuring a single character separately to the rest of the production, in order to minimise the time the set needed to be up, and in any case the sets for the Mullrine's main reception room and the house's entrance hall are continuous, as a glorious tracking shot in Episode Three demonstrates.

[15] *Assigned* 61%

exactly rather than rhetorically. Mullrine's calendar and the party invites specify that the party is being held on Saturday 21 August (were the story to take place in 1981, the 21st would be a Sunday, and the Sunday five days before the transmission of Episode Six at that).

So, again, in a bizarre example of art and life paralleling, rather than imitating, one another, the serial has two timelines; the mad dash for production that is in no way reflected by the lackadaisical traipse to transmission, resulting in a story about drifting back in time that explicitly has to take place more than a year before its first audience could see it. Wholly coincidentally, by the time the serial arrived on television the No 1 selling single in the country was, and would remain for all of its run, Shakin' Stevens cover version of Jim Lowe's 1956 hit 'Green Door'. This curious retro record, which defiantly tried to turn back the clock more than twenty years, is oddly redolent of aspects of *Assignment Five*, where the presence of a green door in 1980 prevents immediate access to the room behind it in 1930, despite a nostalgic attempt to reach the past.

If the audience noticed, no one said. The serial was transmitted at 7pm on Tuesdays and Wednesday, and gathered 17-19% of people watching television at the time, no better and no worse than the previous serials. There was little publicity and little reaction to a story that was something of an oddity even within the very odd series of which it was a part. 'It's not the direction I would have gone in,' commented Hammond of *Assignment Five* in later years, before adding, 'But it's nice to have a variation.'[16]

---

[16] *Counting Out Time*, 23m 29s

The remainder of our discussion of *Assignment Five* will take place in the order in which it was written, transmitted and perhaps (largely) recorded: Episode by Episode. When dealing with a paradoxical series about time, sometimes the best thing to do is go in a straight line.

Assignment Five

Episode One by Don Houghton

'I remember the house was always full of perfect roses,' seventy-four-year-old Emma Mullrine tells her brother Arthur, remembering the summer of 1930 from a distance of fifty years. 'Such an exciting year,' she coos. That she does so ensures *Assignment Five* begins by stating its principal theme, of the dangers and delusions of nostalgic reminiscence, of living in the past. It also lets the audience know from very early on that the, generally sympathetic, Miss Emma's divorcement from the lives of ordinary people is total. Her 'exciting year' of 'perfect roses' is also at the beginning of the Great Depression, as living standards across the West collapsed in the aftermath of the consequences of the Wall Street Crash.

Miss Emma has no excuse for not being aware of this, she was not only alive, she was an adult (we will find out later in this episode that she was 24 that year). More than that, her own financial prosperity, in 1930 and ever since, is a result of her brother Arthur's business acumen and her lover George's inventive brilliance being, between them, enough for their family finances not to be affected by that financial cataclysm. The Great Depression saw millions thrown into poverty not only through no action of their own, but in a way that no action they could possibly have taken would have prevented. Emma, as we shall see as the story continues, is, while charming and pleasant, ultimately self-absorbed to the point where few other people are even real to her.

Producer Shaun O'Riordan, on this serial pulling double duty as producer and director, has noted how strikingly middle-class *Assignment One*'s family are to 21st century eyes,[17] and commented on how this contrasts with the production team's then determination to have the people threatened during the course of Sapphire and Steel's adventures be 'ordinary'. The phlegmatic pensioner and hobbyist Tully in *Assignment Two* and the occupants of the grotty boarding house in *Assignment Four* qualify better as 'ordinary' than the Jardine family, with their enormous house on what seems to be a private island, but in *Assignment Five* we find ourselves not even in the company of well-heeled professionals, but instead in the home of one of the very upper middle class.

Steel's alias for penetrating this world is 'The Honourable Miles Cavendish', indicating that the persona he is adopting (or the person he is impersonating, it is unclear if there is a real Miles) is of someone who is the son of a Baronet, a Viscount or an Earl. An aristocrat, or at least the son of a member of the House of Lords. Arthur Mullrine, though goes one better, and is – at least in the nineteen eighty sections – actually a Lord himself; a peer of the realm.

Yes, it is made clear that he has been given, not inherited this title, and that it is a recognition of his pre-eminence as a businessman, but it is also clear that, even before Mullrine and McDee's money making adventures in the 1930s, the Mullrines at least were particularly well heeled. Their house is essentially the same in 1930 and 1980, and this is not simply a matter of avoiding redressing sets: the Mullrines have clearly long had money. Felix Harborough talks of Mullrine as a younger man 'Hell bent on making a second

---

[17] Commentary 1:1 2m35s

fortune for the Mullrine family' and it is a 'second fortune', not a **replacement** one; there is no implication that the Mullrines or McDee's lost money in the depression, despite Arthur's personal experience of the Wall Street Crash.

The victims of Time (or 'It' as Sapphire and Steel call their offscreen antagonist in these six episodes) are people who are, in the normal course of things, immune to outside threats, immune even to the greatest economic meltdown of their century, except as a spur to greater profit. This makes sense, because in this story, unlike any other **Sapphire & Steel** serial, they are in peril because of deliberate action by a human being, in this case Miss Emma (although we will not discover this until Episode Six).

Yes, the story's true villain is an abstract something which is presumably sufficiently anthropomorphised to be able to communicate, and make a bargain, with Emma and which may (or may not) be an avatar for Time itself, but it is kept offscreen, leaving its avatar and co-conspirator to do what talking and explaining there is to be done. The threat to everyone in the serial is ultimately a lonely little old lady, and the story's concerns are human, rather than abstract. Lost love and loneliness are the problem here, not the unintended danger of nursery rhymes or a monster's ability to use photochemical processes against human beings.

It is appropriate then, that almost as soon as the story has started, and long before we understand the complicated Interrelationships of the Mullrines and their associates in two different time zones, the squabbling over memory begins. Not just with Emma's fatuous observation about roses, but also over the memory of the late, lamented George McDee. We know little of George at this point, but watch as his widow and a woman we do not yet know was his lover argue over whether he liked parties, or was fond of the house they are standing in. As they do so a portrait of the man himself looms large over them, just as it seems McDee himself has loomed over this extended family in the not-yet-specified number of years since his death.

Arthur Mullrine is proud of the company that he and McDee built, so much so that emotion rises in his voice as he recalls their early successes, so much so that he is determined to mark the firm's 'fiftieth year of operation' with a party that pretends to take place in their **first** year of operation, with guests instructed not simply to dress 'in period' but also to refrain from wearing artificial materials, such as polyester[18], that did not exist in 1930.

Exactly what Mullrine is marking, and how, is not entirely clear from the serial itself. Was there a party at Mullrine's house on this night, on 21st June, in 1930? If so, what was it celebrating? Partial answers, some contradictory, will be revealed over the course of *Assignment Five*, but it's enough in the context of Episode One to say that Mullrine has invited his sister and half a dozen friends and colleagues to his home to pretend for an evening that it is fifty years ago on that very night, and that he has gone to considerable trouble and expense to assist them in that affectation.

A case in point is Mullrine's 'trick' with the tape recording of a long-ago cricket commentary hidden in the back of an ancient wireless. This begins to play as Howard McDee turns the radio on in the hope of finding out the score in a cricket game being played in the

---

[18] Invented in 1941.

real world in 1980[19]. Obviously, it exists as an example of both the jokes Mullrine will play on his guests and of the lengths he has gone to in order to recreate 1930 for them. It also allows the moment, several minutes later, where the back is again removed from the wireless to reveal the valves one would expect to find in a pre-war radio[20].

In what may be a deliberate touch, the details of the cricket match being reported on are wrong. Yes, the first Test of the 1930 Australian cricket tour of England was indeed at Trent Bridge, but it took place 13-17th June, with no cricket played on 21st and at no point during the Trent Bridge test were Australia 123 for 1[21]. Yet the personnel listed for the game are accurate, and the choice of Don Bradman and Wally Hammond as the batsman and bowler playing as the radio is turned on is interesting in itself, at least in so much as it invokes the intense personal rivalry between the two players which, unusually for cricket, seems to have drifted into personal animosity. This is, after all, a story about a silly game which becomes deadly serious. (It may also be relevant that Wally Hammond shares his surname with **Sapphire & Steel**'s creator, whom this is the first episode of the series without.)

---

[19] On June 21 1980 England were playing the West Indies at Lord's. Howard wants to know 'How Boycott is getting on'. He was caught out for an atypically low 8. As this match would have already taken place by the time the scene was recorded, this may be a deliberate joke.

[20] Felix's comment after Mullrine's subterfuge is revealed that his party trick was 'All done with mirrors!' feels like another nod to Agatha Christie, whose most celebrated novels include *They Do It with Mirrors* (1952) and *The Mirror Crack'd from Side To Side* (1962), the latter of which was being made as a big budget film in the summer of 1980, and was much in the news. It would be released just before Christmas that year.

[21] http://www.espncricinfo.com/wisdenalmanack/content/story/151745.html

The story the commentator tells of Hammond catching a swallow after mistaking it for a ball in flight seems to be not so much apocryphal as without precedent, and certainly not part of the mythology of Hammond's career. If this was invented by Houghton, rather than inserted by him in error, it is worth wondering what he meant by it. It is perhaps an oblique reference to the proverb of one swallow not making a summer, which would nicely dovetail with some of the story's other concerns.

That the date Mullrine is trying to recreate in his party is June 21st, and that this is, as he notes, the summer solstice, could be seen as tapping into the 1970s vogue for Folk Horror[22]. This subgenre, usually concerned with the past reaching out to damage, overwhelm or destroy the present (or at least the characters' present) might seem a natural categorisation for **Sapphire & Steel**. Yet while *Assignment One* invokes nursery rhymes, folk myth and the political-military conflicts of the mid to late sixteenth century, little in *Assignments Two* to *Four* or *Six* really follows on from that initial story.

Getting dark before seven o'clock in the evening, which is what happens here as the cricket is discussed, is the antithesis of what should happen on the longest day of the year, even somewhere with as mercurial summers as England. (Although Felix does dismiss the bad weather as exactly what one would expect in an unpredictable English summer.)

---

[22] The term was not actually used in the 1970s, being a retrospective application not be coined until the next century, albeit the term originates with Piers Haggard, director of *The Blood on Satan's Claw*, and thus a key figure in any movement that existed.

By the time Sapphire and Steel arrive in this episode of their own series[23], we are already thirteen minutes in, and they already look wholly out of place in their 1980 clothes and hair. The audience has been seduced, as Mullrine wants his guests to be seduced, into seeing 1930 before 1980, even in a television programme, with its video interiors and studio lighting, that repeatedly accidentally asserts through its technique that 1980 is exactly where it's from.

Sapphire and Steel have a mission (we have been told in *Assignment Three* that the Agents normally receive some kind of brief before engaging) but they are unsure exactly what it is. Going upstairs to change into clothing appropriate to 1930, they worry that the host of the party may have 'started this as a game' and that an undefined 'It' has 'taken over someone downstairs'. It could be 'any one of them,' says Sapphire. 'Or all of them!' counters Steel. Sapphire points out that this wouldn't make sense. That 'there has to be a victim. Or victims.'

This elliptical conversation, like many in the series in which the lead characters discuss their work, gets away with a lot by being between two people, both of whom know the same things. That which is unspoken, which could be revealed to the audience without crude info-dumping, is used to hide that which is unexplained. This extends to the nature of Sapphire and Steel's enemy, the aforementioned 'It' which comes up again and again in such lines as 'why'd 'It' choose this house?' They both know what 'It' is, so neither has any reason to say, except to inform us, and so neither does. Urgency is maintained, tension is created, but clarity is never offered.

---

[23] Steel's voice booming from outside a locked door by way of introduction recalls his first appearance in the first serial.

The closest the series ever gets to really defining the nature of that which Sapphire and Steel fight is in Sapphire's explanation to Robert Jardine in the second episode of the first serial. This must be understood to be partial given that she is not simply explaining to a child but doing so immediately after explicitly confirming to Steel that she will put it to Stephen in simple terms. There, though, time is both the corridor that surrounds all things and the thing that breaks through that corridor when the corridor is weakened by human action or by other factors. That's paradoxical, time seemingly attacking and weakening itself before attacking humans.

P.J. Hammond has often noted that his original title for the series was **The Time Menders**[24] and that implication of healing or fixing or mending, along with the series' opening narration's reference to Sapphire and Steel not being 'transuranic'[25], perhaps ties into this notion of time being both the enemy and the thing the enemy is attacking. Perhaps the best analogy is to some forms of cancer, where the human (or animal) body begins to fight itself.

If so, its extrapolation in this story, if not this episode, is effective, even if it is instinctive rather than deliberate. Here, the threat to the Mullrine family and their guests, and ultimately the whole world, stems from one of their own.

---

[24] E.g. on PJ Hammond and Shaun O' Riordan, DVD Commentary *Assignment One*, Episode One: 11m23s

[25] Transuranic elements are those with a number on the periodic table above 92, they decay radioactively and are usually synthesised or isolated in laboratory conditions, rather than found in nature in the way lower numbered elements, are. See Schell, Cody, **Silver Archive 1b***: Sapphire & Steel Assignments Three and Four* for further discussion of the elements.

Downstairs from Sapphire and Steel's discussions, those guests have already spied through the window a church tower that was bombed out and raised to ground during World War Two. This would seem to give the lie to Felix's assertion to Mullrine that 'you can't make it 1930, you can only pretend.' More, Felix's wife Annabelle finds herself unable to remember what year they are really in. It's here that we first get some idea of the complicated interrelated sex lives of the Mullrines' circle. Annabelle is having an affair with Howard McDee, something that both his grandmother and the Mullrine siblings seem to have noticed, even if Felix has not.

In the opening scene of this episode, we have already had it implied that there exists a sexual relationship between Lord Mullrine and his secretary Miss Shaw[26], via his references to her 'bedroom in the annex' that both, laughing, acknowledge she doesn't need to move through the house to access. There will be more descriptions, if not depictions, of the bedhopping that goes on in this clique in later episodes. For the moment the audience will have to content themselves with Sapphire's ability, on entering the party, to intuit what we already know, using her seemingly inexhaustible telepathic powers, which also tell her, as will become important in the next episode, that the elderly Felicity McDee has been unfortunate to live long to enough bury 'both her husband and her son'.

As the episode comes to a close there are puns on 'fortune', both in the sense of clairvoyance and also as in the kind of which Arthur Mullrine has amassed two, while Felix's comment that Arthur could

---

[26] Houghton had written for the 1970 series of **Doctor Who**, which had a regular character Doctor Elizabeth Shaw, who was usually referred to as 'Miss Shaw' onscreen. The reference may be deliberate or unconscious.

use Miles' (which is to say Steel's) ostensible expertise in 'the futures market' to 'make a killing' foreshadows the murder plot, as does his other observation that 'logically if it was 1930 only you and Emma, and Mrs McDee could be here. The rest of us haven't been born yet.'

As the party progresses, Sapphire and Steel become interested in the electric, computer-assisted door to Mullrine's office, the only part of the drawing room in which they are located which would not have been there in 1930. (We are told Mullrine had it installed in 1938). The 1920s pseudo-science of ley lines, which enjoyed a revival in the 1970s, is invoked as Sapphire and Steel discover that a ley line (here not defined) runs under the door to Mullrine's office. Sapphire seemingly detaches a part of her consciousness to investigate what is happening behind the door, which is suddenly enveloped in both eerie blue light and abstract flames patterns that only she and Steel can see. With Sapphire's behind-the-door consciousness not responding to his telepathically calling her name, Steel begins to panic.

Episode Two by Anthony Read

Both writers of this serial have talked about the fun they had presenting each other with cliffhangers for the other to get out of (Terry Nation and Dennis Spooner said the same thing about their joint 1965/6 **Doctor Who** serial *The Daleks' Master Plan*) so it is something of a disappointment that Anthony Read's first episode opens by comprehensively dismissing the cliffhanger of his co-writer Don Houghton's instalment, reducing its final moments to transitory peril which exists only to provide a cliffhanger.

Once this bit of scripting housekeeping has been negotiated, Read is able to get down to business, with Sapphire's surprising revelation that far from being a place associated with great regret or trauma, Mullrine's office is marked by an extra sensory feeling of **joy**: 'Something wonderful happened in there'. It's a counterintuitive set up, a deliberate contradiction of what regular **Sapphire & Steel** viewers would expect, for what follows over the next twenty or so minutes.

The arrival of Tony Purnell and his girlfriend Veronica Blamey allows this episode, and television viewers who had come to the story with it, to be clear to its audience about the nature of Mullrine's party, and that its own events take place in the present, not pre-war. Like Sapphire and Steel in Episode One they instantly look very out of place. They are both very much late '70s/early '80s 'types', with her flat hair and fading hippy influenced clothing and him with his nasty polyester jacket and white trousers.

Like Sapphire and Steel, they are sent upstairs to change after arriving in 1980 clothes, but unlike the agents they are harried into doing so and criticised for not dressing up before they arrived at the house and thus spoiling the illusion that the party is taking place in 1930. Whether this is a discontinuity between Read and Houghton's speed-written scripts, which do not seem to have been revised with reference to one another (as we'll look at later), or an example of Mullrine's increased agitation (or both) is up to the individual viewer.

Tony and Veronica are an interesting couple. As Sapphire notes to Steel as she reads them, she is keener on him than he is on her, he is rather ruthless and she is 'not very bright'. That latter opinion seems fair, but harsh. Veronica is the only human character, except

Greville, who doesn't seem to be indulging in some kind of secret keeping, or deception of either the audience or her fellow partygoers. (The absolutely guileless way she tries to be seductive when telling Tony about her 1930 nightie is strangely touching.) It is this, as much as her being the youngest of the party and how that feeds into the story's conceit, that means she must be the first one to die.

Tony is a different matter, and there is subtlety in both writing and performance that rather gets lost on a single viewing. Tony is, for example, very nice to the doorman at the Mullrines. He knows his name and asks after a recent illness. This is a bad back, but Purnell still lets the much older man carry his luggage. Sympathy for the lower orders is all very well, but they must know their place. Later he is gratuitously rude to the woman on the end of the telephone the moment she won't do exactly what he wants (he does not know it is impossible). This is the kind of rudeness of which only the specifically well-mannered are capable, the calculated dismissiveness of someone who knows how they should behave.

Like when Purnell admits to being a banker 'born and bred', we see again the inherited nature of the position and power of these people. (This is not an accident, and is brought up on a few other occasions, e.g. 'The Purnells are our merchant bankers,' says Felix indicating a multi-generational family firm, and when Tony attempts his phone call he tries to remember 'Dad's old number at the bank'.) Again, the story is flagging the inherited privilege of its characters. Sapphire, though, gazumps Purnell by asking in her cut glass accent, 'Don't you find all that money awfully tedious?' The attitude of the old aristocracy, of land and long history[27] is contrasted with the relatively new money of a few generations of bankers. Purnell tells Sapphire that money 'has its uses'[28]. But what follows is doubly interesting. He begins to flirt with, and try to impress, her, specifically, going so far as to dance with her[29]. Even for a generational merchant banker and a newly created peer, there are social ladders to climb.

The birthday cake for his company which Mullrine unveils for Veronica to cut is rather like a wedding cake, a point made explicit when it's suggested to her that she imagines it's her own wedding cake. The brief look of resentment, rage and panic that crosses actor Christopher Bramwell's face is an excellent indication of how seriously Tony takes his relationship with Veronica. (The scenes with the shaving brush and the attempts to contact the bank show that Purnell and Blamey have separate rooms, which seems a bit prudish for 1980 if not for 1930 but may also indicate a desire on Purnell's part to reserve his choice of with whom he spends the night until later.)

The cake flags up something else about the story's setting and offers another slight inconsistency. The implication in this episode

---

[27] We have already established that Sapphire's cover's husband is the son of an aristocrat, perhaps the heir to an Earldom or Viscountcy.

[28] Felix's quip about money ('I prefer to know where the next Range Rover is coming from') marks him out as the only member of Mullrine's group with a sense of irony about himself and a sense of distance from their world. It is fitting that as the story develops he becomes the closest thing Sapphire and Steel have to an ally in the house.

[29] Felix dances with Veronica and Felix's wife dances with her lover Howard. Which is about as close to a representation of the, let's face it, swinging, of this group as can be represented on early evening fantasy television.

is that the party is fifty years to the day after another party, and that that party was held to celebrate the start of Mullrine International[30]. (The cake losing its '50th anniversary' decorations but retaining the others as the room shifts back in time might be seen to indicate there was literally another cake in 1930 and that like everything else this has been recreated by Arthur.) Later episodes won't show a party, as such, on that night in 1930, and we are shown that Mullrine's company existed before that date.

This episode is also the first time we are told that McDee died on 22nd June 1930, e.g. fifty years minus a day from the date of Mullrine's anniversary party. This creates the strange implication that not only did McDee die the day after the company that, according to Arthur in Part One, he and Arthur 'built with our own hands' started, but that Mullrine is sufficiently insensitive to throw a party on effectively the fiftieth anniversary of his friend's death and invite his widow. And that she would agree to come. And that neither of them would mention these specifics.

George McDee's arrival is a barnstorming moment, bolstered by the charismatic effortlessness of Stephen MacDonald's performance as McDee[31], and given some weight by Sapphire's emphatic announcement to Steel that McDee is 'not a ghost'. This visitation is due to time travel, not a haunting.

---

[30] This is in keeping with Arthur mentioning in Episode One that he remembers noting that it was the summer solstice 'at the time', i.e. in 1930.

[31] Amusingly, as if keen to flag that McDee is a Scot, writer Read has virtually every sentence McDee says end with 'Is it?' It's an effective rhetorical flutter but so often used that it becomes obvious it's an artefact of the speed with which the script was written.

McDee does not recognise any of the aged versions of his friends and family as themselves. At this point, they appear to him as they appear to us. He does, however, confuse Howard, the grandson he never met, with his son Malcolm. 'He must be the image of his father at the same age,' Sapphire telepathically concludes to Steel and for the audience's benefit. This sort of confusion of similar looking relatives is occasionally used by Agatha Christie[32] but here it causes several wrinkles in the story. Jeremy Child (Howard) was 34 during recording[33] and Stephen MacDonald (George) was forty-eight. If George was the same age as the actor playing him, he was too young to have a son of 34. So, either Malcolm (and Howard) was younger than he looks, or McDee was older than he looks. Or both.

However, we will later discover that in 1930 McDee was having an affair with the 24-year-old Emma. Even if McDee is at the bottom end of his plausible age range, the implication is that he was nearly a generation older than the Mullrine siblings. But what of his wife? Well, Nan Munro, who plays Felicity, was born in 1905. Which would make her character twenty-five in 1930 if she is the same age as the actress playing her. Making her two decades younger than her husband, which is possible, but a decade younger than the man mistaken for her son. Which isn't[34].

It is worth noting that the scene, indeed the episode, does not seem to be written to be delivered under a portrait of McDee. (This

---

[32] E.g. *Hercule Poirot's Christmas*.

[33] Assuming it took place in August 1981.

[34] Of course, actors are not always the same age as the characters they play, e.g. Davy Kaye (Lord Mullrine) was 64 at the time of recording, at least a dozen years younger than his character, but something is awry here.

portrait is required to be on set by the script to Episode One but has not been mentioned in dialogue in Episode Two and it is possible that Read did not anticipate the set having one.) This would explain, or at least justify, how Howard doesn't seem to know who George McDee is, despite him being his grandfather, him addressing him by his father's name, and there being a whacking great portrait of him in the room in which they are standing, which all concerned know to be of George McDee. This could be written off against the idea of McDee being an imposter hired by Mullrine for the purposes of the party, as Felix suggests, but it's not that; Howard does not seem to **recognise** the face of a man with whom he must have been familiar since childhood[35].

The physical resemblance between the father and son McDees, finds both an echo and an inversion in the treatment of Greville the butler here. The first episode has established that Greville is fifty-two, and the final episode will gloss this by letting us know that in 1930 there were two Grevilles in the Mullrine's home, the then-butler and his two-year-old son who would succeed him in his position, and who is asleep in his cot on the night of the fire. Father and son are played by the same actor, Peter Laird.

Laird moderates his performance at points in Episode Two; the older Greville seen in Episode Six will have a stronger accent and a more relaxed manner, both of which are present in a more limited form in the scenes in Episode Two in which Greville arranges Tony Purnell's clothes and expresses confusion about electric razors and telephone exchanges. Father and son are, if not exchanging places,

---

[35] Another oddity here is that Sapphire and Steel have a conversation out loud within a metre or so of the rest of the guests without anyone noticing. Perhaps this was intended to be one of their telepathic exchanges? Nevertheless, they speak out loud.

then combining? Yet it is clearly the younger Greville whom McDee addresses in the main drawing room with the butler as resentful and questioning of who and what McDee is as anyone else in the room. The older Greville would inevitably know McDee (as we see in Episode Six) and it is strange that McDee himself does not recognise a butler who looks almost identical to the house's usual one ('Whoever you may be and whatever your name is...' he says to Greville).

This brings us back, by a circumlocutious route, to Tony Purnell. Once killed off in Episode Three, Tony will play no further part in the story (we do not even see him return to life in Episode Six, time being reset to before his arrival at the house) but his family's long connection with the Mullrines opens the possibility that he too will end up becoming, or at least being mistaken for, his own father as time goes further awry. It is easy to imagine a version of this story where Malcolm McDee and Purnell Senior, as well as the older Greville, are present at the 1930 party in Mullrine's house that we see in Episode Six.

There is also a brief, strange suggestion that Tony is also Malcolm's (biological) son, and thus Howard's half-brother[36] when Felix lets slip while talking to Veronica as both watch Tony chat up Sapphire: 'Tony neglecting you... Takes after his father I'm afraid. Have you met Malcolm yet? I've known him since I was in nappies.' Is this another vanishing subplot or has the writer briefly confused Howard and Tony? It would be in keeping with the 'bedhopping' that goes on in this house in both 1930 and 1980. (As if to make sure we remember this is not a recent thing, Arthur becomes angry when Emma expresses sympathy for the way George treats Felicity.

---

[36] The actors do not look unalike.

'Poor Felicity indeed. Don't be such a hypocrite Emma. It doesn't become you.'.)

Emma's reference to Queen Mary is both oddly overfamiliar and strangely anachronistic. During the lifetime of her husband, King George V, Mary of Teck should be formally referred to as 'the Queen'. Only during the reigns of her sons and later her granddaughter, when she was a Queen Dowager, should she be referred to as 'Queen Mary'. This may be an error on the scriptwriter's part, or it could be another indication that all is not quite well with characters' memories and their understanding of where they are in history. (It does not seem to be the sort of mistake Emma Mullrine would make.) The explanation may lie in Emma's reference to a party at 'Bertie's'. This may be taken as a nod to P.G. Wodehouse's Bertram Wooster, a character of this era, but it could also refer to the then Duke of York, later King George VI, who was known as Bertie. How high do the Mullrines' connections go?

Returning to Mullrine's office, we discover that only a few moments have passed since Mullrine exited the office in 1980, despite at least a few hours passing from the party and the audience's perspective. From Anne Shaw's perspective her scene eight minutes into Part Two follows only seconds from the first scene of Part One.

It is likely then, that the doorbell ring that led to the arrival of Sapphire and Steel was actually Purnell and Blamey arriving, given that time is moving more slowly on the other side of the door, as the room and its inhabitants are dragged backwards to 1930. The scene also serves to demonstrate to the audience that the barrier between 1980 and the party is not permeable from the 1980 side either. As with Purnell and Veronica's clothes, no opportunity to emphasise the sheer 1980-ness of Mullrine's office is spurned, including the camera favouring the computer or electronic adding machine on Shaw's desk.

In the party, Emma Mullrine insists that everyone plays a party game before dinner. As the game of Sardines[37] progresses, Howard McDee searches Tony Purnell's room. Why is this? Obviously, it is to set up something, eventually demonstrated as a red herring itself, in the next episode. But why from Howard's own point of view? Unless it is to suggest that Howard is worried that Purnell is also having an affair with Felix's wife Annabelle?

Whatever the reason, the episode comes to an end as Annabelle finds Veronica dead in a cupboard and screams for help. Nearly an hour into our Agatha Christie pastiche, we've finally had our first dead body.

Episode Three by Don Houghton

With nearly almost exactly two minutes of repeated material from the previous episode and opening titles and a further minute and a quarter of closing titles, there is under twenty minutes of new material here, but almost all of it is extremely interesting.

As we begin, with Annabelle screaming in horror as she discovers Veronica's corpse, it is not her husband Felix to whom she screams for help, but her lover Howard. Is this an indication of who she

---

[37] A variation on Hide and Seek, in which only one person 'hides' and everyone else 'seeks'; anyone who finds the hider must join them in their hiding place, meaning it will become exponentially more cramped, making the hiders packed like tinned fish.

wants with her in moments of extreme stress? Or does she know he's nearer? Is she in on his as yet unexplained casing of upstairs? Once Howard arrives we quickly discover that the conceit of Howard being confused for Malcolm is comprehensively dropped for this episode, raising the possibility it was a grace note added by Anthony Read in scripting Episode Two, and not part of Houghton and Read's original plotting discussions.

The details of that plot are kept open, for a time by Sapphire and Steel's discussion about how the murderer and the party guest possessed by 'It' '...could be one and the same'. **Could** be. Which means it could also **not** be. Later in the episode, Tony Purnell is terrorised by a blue light, not unlike the one that blocked Sapphire's access to Mullrine's office, and responds, 'Oh, it's you' to a shadow that occupies his door at a point where all the other cast members are gathered in the entrance hall to the house. This might be thought to point to a member of the staff as the killer, at least as a red herring.

Greville has already identified the knife that killed Veronica as one of the Mullrines' carving knives and said that he set it out in the dining room. This not quite right. It may be a Mullrine carving knife, but it is also the same knife – or at least the same prop – that Veronica used to cut the cake in the previous episode. This could be another discontinuity between the two writers' scripts smoothed over in production. Or it could be meant to briefly cast suspicion on Greville. The Butler Did It is a cliché of detective fiction[38] that has become loosed from the genre and roams free in common culture. It would be odd to not invoke it at all and the story surely does here.

---

[38] E.g. In 'The Musgrave Ritual' (1893) by Sir Arthur Conan Doyle.

Going by what happens later, the killer and 'It' are separate, but not quite in the way a viewer of Episode Three might assume. Miss Emma's genuine horror at the death of Veronica is not hypocrisy, even though she is, in in the broadest sense, responsible for it. She clearly has no understanding of what 'It' is doing, despite her own deal with 'It'. Its methods are its own. This opens up another idea. 'This is not a damn story! This is real!' insists a furious Howard as Steel talks about the murder; 'Is it?' replies Steel. Given that the first thing he does after this is head to the library, where Sapphire will read a cheap paperback murder mystery[39], he is not being either flippant or rhetorical. He has picked up on Felicity McDee's announcement 'And then there were nine!'[40] The idea is that the entity, time, or 'It' is itself indulging in Agatha Christie pastiche, rather than the authors. This displacement of authorial fiat onto something within the story itself hasn't quite come up in **Sapphire & Steel** before. (The scene in the library returns to the idea of the house being on a ley line[41] last expressed in Episode One, the 'perfect place for turning the clock back,' says Steel without further adumbration.)

It has been noted that Steel is extraordinarily verbose in this episode, especially when compared to his usual, taciturn characterisation. This could be seen as an error on writer Don

---

[39] She reads *Murder Me Twice* by G Drew. This appears to be a fictional book (as opposed to a book of fiction), with the British Library catalogue having no record of a book of that title by an author of that name.

[40] If Felicity can remember the details of *And Then There Were None*, she hasn't reverted to her 1930 self fully as of yet. The book wasn't published until 1939. It also means that she's forgotten her husband isn't dead anymore, as including George there are still ten for dinner.

[41] Here defined as 'A line of increased magnetic activity on the earth's surface'. At this point Steel also again invokes the Summer solstice. Both linking and returning to two ideas that went missing during Episode Two.

Houghton's part, but it is more likely that it is related to the pastiche element of the story. There is some suggestion he is acting out a role rather than following wholly his own instincts, just as the partygoers are. David McCallum's performance is slightly different from usual too; he gives still a slightly different voice and more exaggerated physical movements as he plays detective. It seems a deliberate, rather than accidental, departure.

Like when Annabelle complains that she 'Can't even remember what happened yesterday, I can't even remember coming here', something like this has become necessary at this point in the story. Too much is happening for the characters for them to cope with, what with all the deaths, resurrections and paradoxes happening around them. They are turning, helped by this amnesia, into characters from the genre in which they have found themselves[42].

When Steel quizzes Lord Mullrine about what he did the previous week, he mentions his London club ('The Denver') and going to the theatre, 'the Knightsbridge Tivoli'. Again, all these details are slightly wrong. The Tivoli Theatre on the Strand, not in Knightsbridge (although it was demolished in 1956, which would make it perfect for its use here). The Denver Club is fictional. Mullrine's memories aren't just awry, they're impossible.

As the amnesia takes hold of the characters, what distresses them is interesting. They fret that they cannot remember. 'where I had lunch today' and 'my own car'; again, the script emphasises a slightly empty, moneyed existence. It would have been far more horrifying for characters to, for example, forget the names of their

---

[42] Having, arguably, originally been characters from a different genre entirely.

40

children (and in keeping with the 'moving back in time' idea) but this way we get a strong idea of the characters' lack of inner lives.

This comes to the fore when Sapphire reads Purnell's personality from his empty champagne glass. This isn't just the perfect symbol, it also gives her a chance to deliver a small soliloquy on him: 'Son of a merchant banker, fast cars, expensive clothes, women... money.' (Although it must be said that the slightly wet Purnell does not seem the dominating 'alpha male' this suggests. But perhaps that money has brought all this to this unlikely figure is the point.)

It is because of this that we learn via flashback that Purnell is also sleeping with Anne Shaw. His reported reassurance to her that he can 'easily get rid of her [meaning Veronica]' is a red herring, but an effective one. When in this trance Sapphire hears a gunshot, conventions of television production would have us believe that the shot has already been fired, and that it is this sound which has snapped Sapphire out of the trance; 'Purnell,' she says, 'somewhere in the house,' but something else has happened. When Steel asks 'when?', she replies 'soon'. This is a murder that has not yet taken place. It's a cunning grace note on the many paradoxes with which the story is concerned.

The confusion in time is now a constant matter against which the characters must guard. Steel notes the date of McDee's death only to be rebuked, 'That's today,' and has to remind them 'Yes, today. But fifty years ago.' Later Steel's wondering aloud about the late McDee prompts Lord Mullrine and Felicity McDee to start talking about him in the present tense, and everything changes gear. Characters are now worried again about their 1930s concerns, not

41

the corpse they found in 1980[43], and they have forgotten both being shocked at George's reappearance and forgetting that it happened at all. (There is also something very pleasing about the close up of an ashtray under the Part Two caption in this episode. It's very 1980, but in a way that would have seemed entirely normal in 1980. The casual smoking accidentally emphasises that 1980 is nearer 1930 than it is to today.)

Later, Sapphire uses her powers to manifest McDee from the past in the library, and he and Steel discuss McDee's work with DNA. This conversation, and that McDee understands it, could be taken to be a mistake. Common parlance would suggest that DNA was discovered more than a decade after McDee's death. In fact, Freidrich Miescher first discovered nucleic acid, which he called 'nuclein' in 1869. Miescher's work was built on by Albrecht Kossel, who identified the core components of DNA at the very end of the nineteenth century. What was discovered in Cambridge in 1953 was the double helix structure of DNA. So McDee's knowledge[44], if not terminology, is not outrageously wrong for the period, and can be seen as acceptable dramatic licence. Whether McDee's discoveries could be made in a small laboratory which looks primitive by 1930s standards, and which is inexplicably off the main living room of someone else's house is another matter entirely, and probably one best not interrogated.

---

[43] More oddly, at this point other characters overhear what seems to be Sapphire and Steel's telepathic communication. A strange inversion of the moment in Episode Two where they have a conversation out loud that no one overhears, and which they surely would've commented on had they done so.

[44] There is, however, the odd matter of Steel talking of 'cloning bacteria', but Sapphire earlier talks about a virus, rather than a bacterium.

At the end of the episode Tony Purnell finally dies, the entity seemingly having grown bored of tormenting him. His death is yet another allusion to Agatha Christie. Purnell is killed by a shot from a gun which is too far away from him for him to have pulled the trigger himself, but there is no one else in the room. This is how the Judge commits suicide at the end of *And Then There Were None*.

On seeing Tony's dying body Annabelle yells 'Tony!' in horror. There has been little suggestion that they are familiar with each other up to now, but this could be seen as yet another indication of the musical chairs-like approach to sexual partners of the Mullrine household in 1980. Perhaps this is why, almost out of shot, Felix earlier chastises his wife 'control your appetites darling, and at least try to grow up.'

Episode Four by Don Houghton

Like all episodes of **Sapphire & Steel**, Episode Four of *Assignment Five* has a brief sequence introducing the programme's stars and writers, before an establishing scene which is itself followed by the main title sequence. For the second and any subsequent episodes of a serial, the brief opening scene is a reprise of the cliffhanger of the previous episode.

We've already noted the shortness of Episode Three, but the reprise of its cliffhanger at the start of Episode Four suggests it could have been shorter still. In this context, Felicity McDee's thundering delivery, in close up, of 'And Then There Were Eight!' is obviously the cliffhanger, and Arthur Mullrine's far less dramatic announcement thirty seconds later that 'if you don't pinpoint it quickly there won't be any of us left to care!' a replacement. The echo on his words to increase their drama surely make that point.

(At slightly over 25m this episode is about as long as it could be without overrunning its slot.)

Sapphire and Steel's subsequent conversation about motives for the murders that are being committed in the house is typical of the series in how it confirms certain plot possibilities in as opaque a manner as possible, while also feeding further ideas into the story. Detective story plotting usually involves the elimination of possibilities, narrowing the possible answers to the question 'Whodunnit?' until we are left with the truth. This is, in a sense, the opposite of how **Sapphire & Steel** often works, and here we find the two approaches clashing head on.

We know, we have always known, that 'It' is ultimately responsible for what is happening at Mullrine's house. The ambiguities are about process, rather than motive or opportunity, never mind the identity of the killer. Which is what makes what happens here so interesting. Sapphire insists that the 'motives are irrelevant' and merely 'part of the setting, part of the time change' but this is rather undercut by what we're finding out elsewhere. The party guests, in Sapphire and Steel's absence, discover that Howard has a motive for murdering Tony. Purnell was siphoning money out of his family bank for his own uses, and McDee, having become aware of this, was blackmailing him.

Unfortunately for Howard, Purnell had confessed to his father, who was going to make good all the money on the condition that he go to the police himself. Which would obviously expose Howard to risk of exposure and even prison. The story about this seems to be true rather than an imposition on the partygoers by 'It'. Felix and Mullrine can both recall it from before they came into the house. This puts Tony's comments about 'getting rid' of Veronica in the previous episode in a different light. The murders of both Veronica and Tony have real-world motives, even if they are being committed as part of 'It''s plan.

'It' is, up to a point, assigning murderers and victims based on how these people would act, their actual motives. Sapphire tells Steel that 'It' is 'having to deal with us on more than one level. As Sapphire and Steel, and as Miles and Virginia'. That seems to be true, but perhaps **they** are having trouble dealing with the inhabitants of the house on more than one level as well? Their assignments so far have largely brought them into contact with innocents threatened by 'Time', but it's hard to use this term to describe anyone at Mullrine's party, excluding Veronica.

Yes, they are victims of 'It', but their own lives generate what it uses against them in a way that is not true of, for example, the children of *Assignment One* or the lodgers in *Assignment Four*. This role confusion does seem to carry over into Sapphire and Steel's own interactions; at one point the characters seem to kiss (the camera pulls away). Is this Miles and Virginia's influence? If so, it's another indication of the role strain being suffered by everyone in the house.

SAPPHIRE

Everything else is irrelevant to the central intention.

STEEL

Which is?

SAPPHIRE

The need to retrace the years back to 1930 until time takes a different course.

She's right. They are irrelevant, what they aren't is **random** killings. There's yet more to this: later, in the library, we are treated to Sapphire's attempt to kill herself with the knife while possessed by 'It'. The scene is terrifyingly played by Lumley and a dramatic highlight of the serial. But at first it seems like padding, like the cliffhanger at the end of Episode One. It's not, though, it's probably key to this aspect. If 'It' can force Sapphire, against her own nature and intentions, to attempt to stab herself in the stomach, and make her laugh maniacally while she does so, it can certainly make Purnell kill Blamey or Howard kill Purnell in line with their own interests.

At one point, Emma rises from dinner, and wanders through to the drawing room. As she does so, Mullrine's 1980 electric door to the office becomes the standard door to McDee's 1930 laboratory. As it does so it flags something interesting about the Mullrine/McDee relationship, in relation to their business. After McDee's death, Mullrine continued to use that room as the centre of the empire they'd built together. But it became an elaborate office, and place of business, rather a private laboratory and place of research. Arthur, even in 1980, uses it for covert sexual assignations[45], just as George did in 1930. Arthur has already made clear he knows/knew nothing about the nature of George's work, so how did he continue their company? It seems that after George's death Mullrine

_____

[45] Although Mullrine does not appear to be married, so why the need for secrecy? Perhaps he is a widowed adulterer who has never dropped his old habits?

46

International became the financial firm it presents as in Episode One, Arthur substituting his own skills for McDee's, just as he imposed his office on George's laboratory. Given that we will later find out that this is where George died, and Arthur knows this, this is a fascinating act, and the electronic door that only Mullrine himself can open a brilliant symbol of how he has shut away the past.

We are in that past as Emma heads to the laboratory. The defocused lens when Emma passes through the house, along with the 'sexy' music that plays as Emma visits George help sell that the character is a young woman visiting a lover, but they only assist what Patience Collier's performance, her body language suddenly all juvenile, her smile suddenly girlish, makes real. Collier was seventy when this serial was made, and it is to her extraordinary credit that her declarations of love and coquettish behaviour do not seem absurd or out of place[46]. Unusual, yes, there's no makeup or dressing changes to indicate that Emma is twenty-four, but we believe that she is, even though the actress playing her is seventy. Interestingly, Stephen MacDonald (George) was nearly fifty when these scenes were shot. As Collier's character is meant to be twenty-four in 1930 (although we continue to see her as she is in 1980), this inverts the age difference between the performers. She is now twenty-five years his senior, not the other way around.

In parallel to this scene we another in the room that George replaced it with. The clock behind Anne again demonstrates that five or six minutes only have passed in 1980, despite hours passing

---

[46] The way Emma plays with the Bunsen burner on George's desk is inspired. It's impish, making Emma seem girlish despite the actress' own age, while the ebbing and flaring of the flame is as good as symbol of their passionate love affair as anyone could wish for.

within the party. Again, the 'modernity' of the office is emphasised, this time through some business with computerised records of Mullrine's family history. These are interfered with by spectral forces; 'It' changes a word in the newspaper report, knowing that Sapphire and Steel will research here – an effective bit of visual storytelling[47], showing us that 'It' is actively engaged in a battle of wits with the agents, deliberately trying to confuse them, without anyone saying this out loud. It also conveniently allows the viewer to skip from the beginning to the end of the characters' dinner, straight from pre-dinner drinks to the port and cigars[48].

Is Howard's announcing that there is an 'Impenetrable barrier' around the house in the same breath that he complains that 'most the servants have left' meant to be surrealism? Or is it another indication of how quickly these scripts were written[49]? It does open the interesting idea that another version of this story is happening downstairs at the Mullrine's. If the servants are all killing each other off from real world motives, but in backwards chronological order from date of birth — which is the logical extrapolation of the

---

[47] The records indicate that George McDee was in possession of a doctorate, and also that he was a physicist. (Although his research is more in the realms of biology or chemistry.) Yet he is always addressed as 'Mister McDee' throughout the story. It is possible that McDee has qualified as a surgeon following his medical degree, which would mean he was entitled to revert to the honorific 'Mister' under archaic UK tradition.

[48] At the end of this scene, we can see the drawing room set through the door of Mullrine's office, indicating the sets are further interlinked than even the long slow pull outs of Episode Three did.

[49] 'Thank you, Malcolm!' says Felicity McDee to Howard at one point, briefly reviving an idea that has lain dormant since Episode Two. Is it possible this is an actorly addition? At the end of the episode George McDee will yell 'Who are you?' at Howard. Clearly in this episode he at least does not mistake his grandson for his son.

reason for their disappearance and how 'It' has achieved it, then it would have been rather nice to see it.

It's a missed opportunity, but there are some interesting grace notes in this episode which are worth acknowledging. There is another clever juxtaposition of shots that again throws suspicion on Greville as he, smiling, lowers his hand to the table just before we see the gun. That gun, though, is now with Sapphire and Steel, but just a moment before it looks as though he has laid his hand on it. Felix talks to Howard of the law putting 'a rope round your neck'. Capital punishment was abolished in Britain[50] in 1969, having been suspended half a decade before. But then the characters might believe they are in 1930 as this conversation takes place. Felix also makes a comment about his wife being hungry despite the murders, 'Annabelle's appetites thrive on crisis,' which seems to acknowledge their argument perhaps being about sex in the previous episode. Superstition is invoked again, with young McDee's horror that Steel might pass the port bottle anti-clockwise[51], and a further discussion of the summer solstice. Humans have 'very little control over our fates on the night of the twenty first,' we are told, something that George McDee disputes. Which, given that he's a sort of ghost, and the whole story is about how he has no choice but to die that night, is really rather marvellous. The way Emma's fatuous declaration that what is going on in the house is down to 'a dear little poltergeist,' is juxtaposed with Steel trying to stop Sapphire stabbing herself is horrific, and

---

[50] It remained in force in Northern Ireland until 1973.
[51] This is considered to be bad luck by tradition, although no one is sure of the origins of this superstition. Suggestions have included that it originated in the Navy, where the port side of the boat is on your left if you are facing the bows, or that it came about to allow the right-handed drinkers to keep their sword-hand free.

genuinely unnerving[52]. The cobwebs on the dinner table as it is accelerated through time[53] suggest another literary antecedent, Dickens' *Great Expectations* (1861).

The episode ends as it begins, in the dining room with a murder. Howard McDee's berating of his family firm for the money they will make from human misery is a key moment in the story. Comparisons are often made between *Assignment Five* and the so-called 'Time Plays' of J.B. Priestley, especially the most famous (and frequently adapted for film and television) *An Inspector Calls* (1945). The earlier *Time and The Conways* (1937) is, however, perhaps a better comparison. The first act is set in the Conways' house in 1919, the second in the same room in 1937, and the third moments after the conclusion of the first, again in 1919. This structure means that the audience sees consequences before actions, blurring cause and effect, and creating multiple juxtapositions, ironic, comic and tragic, between what the characters believe will or did happen, and what does.

Both plays, and others by Priestley, reflect his own socialist convictions, and are intended to force the audience to consider the impact that their actions have in the world, not just on the people they know and interact with, but on the rest of society[54]. Howard's rant here has a little of that and does seem to set the scene for the

---

[52] It may also point to the way that 'It' made contact with Emma in the first instance, or at least be her revealing her opinion of the creature with which she has struck a deal. After all, it has promised to save her long dead lover and restore her youth. Why shouldn't she find it 'dear'?

[53] 'This is as it would have been if it had lain here for fifty years,' says Sapphire.

[54] Inspector Goole's final speech in *An Inspector Call* is the clearest, most famous and perhaps also least subtle example.

final two episodes in which the unintended effects of human actions will come very much to the fore.

The only problem with it is that it seems very much out of character, especially at the end of the episode where we've found out that he is indulging in a spot of blackmailing of one of that firm's bankers. Is this 'It' speaking through him, as it acted through Sapphire? Her comment, as she goes to shoot Steel, 'I'm not sorry about this,' seems calculated, like Howard's attack on his family, to cause the maximum amount of distress to those that hear it before they die.

Dear little Poltergeist, indeed!

Episode Five by Anthony Read

As Howard McDee collapses on the dining table, it's up to the ghost[55] of his grandfather, of all things, to take the lead in trying to revive him, or at least ascertain that he's definitely dead. He pushes his way to the front, pointing out that he's the only doctor in the room. 'I've always warned him about drinking stuff like this!' says George McDee during his brief examination. This must mean that, as in Episode Two, he is seeing Howard as Malcolm. That this follows on from the pre-credits sequence taken from the previous episode in which he snarls 'Who are you?' at the same man, is rather odd, and could be seen to confirm the idea that the Malcolm/Howard confusion is essentially limited to Anthony Read's episodes of the serial; especially when Felicity begins to refer to the body as 'my son' rather than 'my grandson'. (Seemingly believing

---

[55] Or whatever he is.

she is her 1930 self, she makes a veiled accusation towards Miss Emma, indicating that she is aware of George's infidelity with her.)

The conversation that follows is about motives for killing Howard, as the survivors grapple with what is happening to them. However, the older members of the party quickly stop taking part, as they rapidly lose their grip on the immediate past, regressing again to people at a party in 1930; the conversation ends when George McDee leaves through a door that has been locked onscreen, and to which Annabelle has the key. Annabelle briefly comes to the fore here, and Jennie Stoller, who has previous been confined to sly comments and looking glamorous, enables a rising sense of panic across her and Felix's conversation with Sapphire and Steel.

We are told, although it is obvious, that Annabelle is much younger than her husband, but this makes us realise that Annabelle must logically be older than Howard, which scarcely seems plausible (Stoller is two years younger than Jeremy Child who, despite his name, could never be considered a young-looking actor). We also discover that Felix was born in 1931[56], meaning that the moment he dies the movement back to 1930 will have been completed.

The moment when Annabelle dies is genuinely horrifying, and all the more so for her husband having a sudden lapse into the manic atmosphere of the 1930 party and joining the older characters in chatting about cars. Completely alone and obviously terrified, Annabelle is electrified by the door handles of the drawing room. The sound effects and the manner in which Jennie Stoller plays it,

---

[56] 'Young man, whoever you are,' Arthur says to Felix casually at one point, indicating his grip on the present has now vanished.

her body jerking and flailing as she collapses to the floor, is really strong for **Sapphire & Steel**'s time slot.

It's Greville the butler who discovers the electrical wires leading from the fuse box to the door handles, transporting the current that has killed her. The way these scenes are played, particularly the period when Greville is alone, make it unlikely that it was he who set up the trap[57], although Peter Laird's sinister delivery of 'meant for your wife' while showing the wires to Felix does help sustain the possibility that 'the butler did it' a little longer. Other things in this episode work towards that conclusion as well. Steel notes that Greville went out through the locked door like McDee and the other 1930 guests and becomes suspicious that the butler is older than he looks and is hiding something, and subsequently sends Felix to interrogate Greville for him. But Steel is wrong. Greville left through a different door entirely, the dining room's service door, not the one Annabelle locked.

Having confessed to Felix's question that they are 'a kind of interplanetary police force,' and introduced the concept that 'time is not as rigid a concept as most people would believe,' Sapphire and Steel explain to him about 'It' and its plan to move the house back in time fifty years and how 'to be consistent, everyone who wasn't born then has had to be eliminated'. 'You call that a rational explanation?' Felix responds tartly. It must be said that actor Jeffrey Wickham's performance throughout this serial is superb. What is asked of him in this scene alone, moving from distraught at the death of his wife, to hostile enquiry, to rational sceptic to helping hand flirting with Sapphire is gargantuan, and Wickham does it all with great sincerity, while keeping Felix likeable at all

---

[57] Unless 'It' made him both do it and forget that he did it.

53

times. (The sheer unconvincing theatricality of how Felix says 'I'm tired, I'll go to bed' when instructed to lie by Steel serve as proof.)

When Sapphire demonstrates her powers to Felix in order to convince him of the truth of what Steel says, she materialises Howard as a ghost at the dining table. It's an odd choice. Why Howard, for whom Felix has no respect? Who the audience know is a blackmailer with a motive for murder? Nevertheless, good material is eked out of the scene as Howard explains he's in some sort of netherworld, spying on his own past: 'I've learned more up here than I ever did down there,' he says, rather soulfully.

Brass, Sapphire's codename for Felix when he is imbued with minor elements of the agents' power, is particularly inspired. The opening narration tells us that Sapphire and Steel and their fellow agents are elements[58]; Brass however is an alloy, a mix of the two elements copper and zinc. The implication is that the agent Brass is a mix of the human Felix and the unearthly powers of Sapphire and Steel. (Steel has acknowledged that they are alien 'in an extra-terrestrial sense' in this episode already. Lumley for her part saw Sapphire and Steel as working for 'a greater power'[59] and considered the voiceover in the opening titles to be the 'voice of God'[60].) The sheer delight on Felix's face when his newly granted telepathy works for the first time is another lovely piece of acting from Wickham.

Again, there are smart grace notes here. The dip back in to 1930s financial values as Mullrine, Greville, Sapphire and Felix play Bridge.

---

[58] They're not, but go with it, and see Schell, *Assignments Three and Four*, for further discussion of this.
[59] *Counting Out Time* 6m15s
[60] *Counting Out Time* 7m 27s

Sapphire's caustic 'they have so many ways,' when asked how humans kill each other. The 1930 Arthur, supposedly a businessman of some vision, seeing airships (rather than aeroplanes) as the future of travel (a nice historical irony of the kind common in period drama, but here serving to suggest that Arthur might not be quite the great businessman he seems). There is also a fine example of Chekov's Gun[61] with the radio, untouched since it was ripped open in Episode One, when Steel manipulates its damaged innards to emit a frequency that will open the door in the absence of Mullrine's electronic handset.

He has to do this in order to access Mullrine's office and 1980. When he arrives there, the office clock tells us that it is 6:40, meaning that less than ten minutes have passed since the first episode began and fewer than five since Anne Shaw saw McDee's ghost. In fact, she's still sitting at her desk, slightly traumatised by that experience, and initially worries that Steel may be a ghost. He isn't, but he is his usual taciturn self and his failure to treat Miss Shaw with any respect at all means he fails to get the information he wants out of either Miss Shaw or the computer.

This means he has to leave and return with Sapphire, who uses different techniques, charming and distracting Miss Shaw, apologizing for her 'husband'. At this stage it is hard to see a reason for this taking place over two scenes rather than one, and a certain amount of padding is evident. It is certainly not Steel's intention to

---

[61] **Chekov's Gun** is a dramatic principle that states that each element in a story must have a function, and if it does not, then it should be removed. The phrase comes from a letter sent to a friend in 1889 by Russian playwright Anton Chekhov (1860-1904) who wrote "If in the first act you have hung a pistol on the wall, then in the following one it should be fired. Otherwise don't put it there."

fail and then return with Sapphire as a kind of bad cop/good cop routine. Nevertheless, it works effectively as one, and also as an illustration of how the characters function, and how they achieve their mission objectives[62].

As with the recruiting of Felix and the tacit admission of more information about their background than in the previous serials, this overt illustration seems like something resulting from the series now being written by someone less unorthodox than Hammond. It's as if Read and Houghton are unconsciously flattening **Sapphire & Steel** out into a multi-authored television series, like **Doctor Who**, rather than the odd auteur project it has been up until now. Of course, they literally have to, in order to write it themselves, but the end result is to turn Sapphire and Steel into something more approximating the leads of a television programme; when written by Hammond they seem more like figures out of a dream.

Felix's Steel-prompted conversations with Mullrine offer interesting details on the state of the Mullrine household and business empire in 1930. We learn that both Emma and Felicity advised Arthur **against** taking George McDee on as a partner. Which might imply that she was the Mullrines' friend before she was George's wife. But then why would she have shares in Arthur's company before she was the wife of his business partner? Perhaps Arthur's chronology is muddled, he has just been dragged five decades back in time, but it's another layer of complexity, or at least complications, in the interrelations of these two families.

---

[62] 'There's a handle on this side,' advises Miss Shaw brightly as they exit. There wasn't in Episode Two. Or at least there was, but it wouldn't work without Mullrine's electronic opener. It's an odd discontinuity and one without any seeming plot or thematic point.

The scene that follows this, as Felix manages to enter the laboratory in 1930 in Arthur's company, is extremely unsettlingly directed, with a vertiginous feeling as Felix accepts Arthur's offer to meet a dead man in a room that isn't there anymore. That acceptance costs Felix his life as he comes into contact with cultures related to McDee's work. Dying, he rushes back to the library to tell Steel what he has discovered. He has been useful, despite Steel only recruiting him as a distraction.

Felix crashes to the floor, dead, after a moment of jet black comedy as Steel bellows 'Not now Felix!' at the dying man trying to warn him, his face covered in (effectively disgusting) disease make up. More than any character since the innocent Veronica, the audience is hit quite hard by Felix's death. This obscures the final Agatha Christie in-joke of the episode.

Five episodes in, there's a body in the library.

Episode Six by Anthony Read

The explicit and implicit influence of detective fiction on *Assignment Five* has been touched on earlier. There are, however, other significant influences on the serial, most noticeably touches of co-writer Don Houghton's own scripts for two of the lesser remembered Hammer **Dracula** films, *Dracula A.D. 1972* (1972) and *The Satanic Rites of Dracula* (1973). Elements of these films utilised here include the infected spores of a man-made disease that can wipe out all life on earth, and the consuming of these in cleansing fire at the conclusion. These influences are most explicit in Episode Six, which Houghton did not write, so they must have come to the story during the writers' joint planning stage. (It is scarcely credible that they should appear in the serial and Houghton not notice.)

57

After the padding and wheel spinning of the previous episode, this final episode moves quickly, and has a lot to fit in. It's probably unavoidable. Arriving in 1930 is the perfect cliffhanger for Episode Five. Had it occurred earlier (say at the Episode Five advert break) it would not have had nearly so much impact. Now we are in 1930, any pretence of Miles and Virginia Cavendish has gone. Sapphire and Steel are now completely themselves, and for no reason which is articulated, invisible to the inhabitants of the house, except when they wish to be. In a neat inversion of the detective story, they are now detectives racing to ensure a murder takes place, even though they are unsure of the killer, only the victim, who is both alive and dead.

What is unusual about this, is that at no point before this has it been confirmed, even suggested really, that McDee was *murdered*. But here it is treated as an established fact from the outset. We have always known George died. And slowly been introduced to when, and where and roughly how. But no one has told us he was *killed*. That he was has slipped into the story without being overtly flagged, presumably due to the speed of its composition. When viewing the serial straight through now (something no one working on it could have conceived of then, of course) this is strikingly odd, and the episode's rush to establish possible motives for McDee's murder is slightly disorientating. And in a different way to how the series usually is. For a while at least Sapphire and Steel are no longer concerned with who has killed everyone else, or who is possessed by 'It' or may have done a deal with it, instead they trying to find out who did or who *will* murder George McDee.

Motives are set up quickly and means and opportunities even quicker. It initially feels, when Felicity nearly shoots George and then can't, that this is the traditional detective fiction double bluff, especially given Sapphire's absolute certainty in the moment. But Sapphire is wrong and we move on. The moment when Arthur nearly stabs George also seems wrong. It's a bit too extreme for their relationship as depicted. Okay, it's only a paperknife, but it's an affectation too far at this point in the story. (And we are specifically meant to believe this could be the moment McDee dies.)

Arthur's motive for killing George would be that George has decided, now his affair with Emma has blown up in his face, to withdraw from his contract with Mullrine allowing them to jointly share in the profits from McDee's inventions. Presumably he is trying to save his marriage[63] by completely removing it from the Mullrine's ambit. There is some self-justification in McDee going to Arthur to demand his agreement back. He reprimands Arthur for 'using his own sister' to tempt him, and Arthur has to correct him, telling him that Emma is genuinely in love with him. That's something we understand now, knowing that she will pine for him for fifty years and what she has done in order to try to get him back.

By this point Emma has already told Arthur 'You've got what you wanted. Now it's my turn. I will have him.' Something that has clearly been her defining aim throughout the story, and the fifty years she's lived between what we see in the last episode and what we have already seen in the first.

Because, yes, it is Emma who is both George's (accidental) killer in 1930 and the person who has arranged everything we have

---

[63] Both men's horrified reaction to the idea of a divorce scandal nicely show that this is 1930, not 1980, and contrast well with the borderline 'swinging' that goes on in this group in the latter decade.

witnessed in order to change that. It might be argued that the revelations as to what the Mullrine and McDee families went through on the night of 21st and 22nd June 1930 are such that their close association for fifty years after the event is implausible. We know from Episode One that Felicity McDee retains her shares in the company her husband set up with Arthur Mullrine[64], and her grandson, not yet born in 1930, is himself a shareholder and familiar with both the old man and his home.

Perhaps it is, like the story's notes about inheritance, nostalgia and money, a comment on the attitudes of the moneyed upper middle classes, bound together by that money and ambition, despite each other, and there is maybe something to unravel here in what the characters do not say. Felicity is shocked by Emma's suggestion that George is guilty of adultery here and devastated when George admits it. Whereas in Episode Three she pointedly says 'I know' to Emma, in context we can take that as being purely about the affair, and a discontinuity with this episode, but what if it isn't? What if 1980 Felicity McDee meant something entirely different when she told Emma Mullrine, 'Never forget, I *know*.'

She's not her 1930 self telling her rival that she knows she is sleeping with her husband, she's her 1980 self reminding her that she was there when she killed him. That their entire lives since have been built on this foundation. George's work. Arthur's money. The silence they have shared. We know from Episode One that Young Greville is devoted to Lord Mullrine, but it can hardly be a

---

[64] 1930 Arthur's enthusiastic speech about how his company will 'Go public' and how 'Mullrine Imperial will become Mullrine International' does paper over some of the logistical cracks of the Mullrine/McDee relationship and history introduced in earlier episodes.

coincidence that the only other witness[65] to any other part of these murderous events, the ignoring of which is the foundation of a business empire, seems to have arranged a job for life for his less able son[66].

The way that, as the laboratory burns down around him and with his supposed friend George lying dead or dying on floor, Arthur risks severe burns to pick up the gun that Emma has killed George with could be seen to indicate that the canny Mullrine is already thinking of the coverup. We know this gun will be given to George McDee's son, Malcolm, who will bequeath it to his own son, Howard. It's hardly likely that either man knew it was the weapon with which their family patriarch was murdered. But Felicity *does* know this. The family heirloom is also evidence. Her family's possession of the gun that killed her husband a constant reminder to the Mullrines of what she knows and what ties them together.

That event, when we see it, is very different from what Felicity or Arthur or perhaps even Emma will remember, either the first or second time they live those five decades between the two parties. Emma has been lied to[67], tricked. She can save George; he and she can be together for the rest of their lives. But the rest of their lives will be almost no time at all, George having accidentally created and incubated a virus that will destroy all life on Earth, and which

---

[65] 'Greville witnessed it!' says Mullrine in another context, but by the end of the story it feels like a nod.

[66] The elder Greville works on Mullrine's contracts, and we see him correcting his employer's mistakes as they do the books. The younger's duties seem more like fetching and carrying, we know he doesn't run the household, as we are told Emma does.

[67] Steel: 'Time is tricking you.' Emma: 'Who is Time?' Sapphire: 'Our enemy. Your enemy' is as close to an explanation as we'll get. It's above average for the series.

will escape with him if he ever leaves his laboratory, and it is not burned to the ground. It's fitting that George McDee, a flawed man but one motivated by a desire to eradicate disease, takes the lead in these last moments[68]. It's really incredibly touching how George talks Emma into setting history right and when he asks her, 'would you have me be the man who destroyed the human race?' we see a kind of human motivation that rarely comes into the programme in which it appears. It is incredibly brave of him, and yet more brave of her, to agree to go through everything, the last fifty miserable years alone, again.

As noted, Hammond's original title for Sapphire and Steel was **The Time Menders**[69]. But it is only here, in the story that he didn't write, that his leads seem to actually fix anything. Time is defeated, the time break is disabled. Nobody needs to die, except George Mullrine, and he has already been dead half a century, and at least the story's conclusion makes his early death a heroic choice of his own, not an accident. 'This is where we came in,' Sapphire says as time restarts, and they are again in their 1980 clothes which seem absolutely wrong in the environs of Mullrine's house. That's the last original dialogue in the story, the rest is repeats from Episode One. It's curiously fitting, and perhaps deliberate, that this is how the only writers other than PJ Hammond to contribute to his series take their leave. Were one inclined, for some bizarre reason, to enforce a 'Hammond Canon' on the series, this story doesn't really

---

[68] Sapphire takes Steel's hand and leads him away as George and Emma talk. This isn't just to give them privacy, it's that it is the humans, not the agents, who solve this one. The human element, not the elements, if you prefer.

[69] E.g. on PJ Hammond and Shaun O' Riordan, DVD Commentary *Assignment One*, Episode One: :11m23s

quite happen whether you do or do not include it. It's a self-sealing loop. Or is it? As we'll see in the next chapter, the story exerts considerable influence, conscious or otherwise, over the only one written after it.

Assignment Five may not be the direction that P.J. Hammond would have taken the series in at this point, had he been able to continue writing it, but it is, as Felix Harborough says of the mercurial aging financial whizzkid turned peer of the realm in whose house of secrets it takes place, really very clever and far richer than most people imagine.

Assignment Six

1: 'Answer to a Higher Authority'

At some point near the end of 1980, the cast of **Sapphire & Steel** assembled to make what would be the series' final serial. Did they know they were working on the characters' last outing? In recent years, Joanna Lumley has intimated that all involved suspected it would be. Hammond, at least, she's suggested[70], knew that no further episodes would be commissioned, and so had made a decision to give the series a memorable send-off within the fiction. David Collings has suggested that another series was on the cards, perhaps with Silver being present in most episodes, but that this plan quietly collapsed around the time the sixth serial was recorded[71].

The three serials the cast and crew had made in such a rush earlier in the year had not yet been screened. The first two would debut in the new year, the third — as we've already seen — would crawl out over Summer 1981, traditionally a period where little new television was scheduled, the three broadcasters choosing instead to show repeats, on the grounds that summer weather meant that few people watched whatever was screened, regardless[72]. Being treated as such by ATV and/or the ITV network hardly seemed a show of confidence. But, as was always the case in Sapphire and

---

[70] *Counting Out Time*, 24m00s

[71] http://www.kaldorcity.com/people/dcinterview.html

[72] The late 1970s had seen a string of exceptionally good summers, which had helped this behaviour 'bed-in' as standard broadcasting practice.

Steel's own adventures, larger forces were at work than were necessarily immediately obvious.

The company that made **Sapphire & Steel** was ATV, the franchise holder for Independent Television in the English Midlands under the now obsolete Federal ITV structure[73]. During the 1980 franchising round it had agreed to make drastic changes to its business operations in order to hold onto the contract. January 1982 would be a substantially new company with a new name and on-air identity: Central. What may also be relevant is that David Reid, **Sapphire & Steel**'s executive producer, internal champion and the man who had bought the series to ATV in the first place, was in the process of moving to the BBC, where he would become the Head of Drama Series and Serials. This serial's director David Foster has intimated that Margaret Matheson, the new Head of Drama at Central, held that ATV's drama had been too flippant and too little engaged with the real world[74]. That's possible, but it's an odd charge to level at a fantasy adventure serial for children and families[75].

It is perhaps more likely that, quite simply, a new broom sweeps clean. Only the most successful and popular ATV series would survive the broadcaster's transformation into Central, and **Sapphire**

---

[73] The 1990 Broadcasting Act made possible a variety of changes in the nature of the ITV network, which consolidated into essentially a single national company devoid of regional identities, beyond local news, by 2002.

[74] *Assigned* 72%.

[75] Matheson had worked on **Play for Today** for the BBC, where her credits included *Abigail's Party* and the original version of *Scum*, the first of several projects with Alan Clarke. Her later career also largely consists of socially conscious drama concerned with issues.

& Steel was not a priority. ('I had an idea,' Hammond acknowledges. 'Things were changing at ATV. Various different people were going to be in power'[76].)

It could also hardly have been said to have dominated the television charts. While popular with children, the recipient of some merchandising[77] and a comic strip in *Look-In*, the 'Junior TV Times' of the era, it only ever achieved around 20% of the available viewers, a poor showing for the dominant channel in terms of ratings in an era of only three stations. Moving the series to 8pm for the third serial was probably a mistake (although understandable given the content), the later slot being more valuable to ITV in terms of advertising and thus innately requiring more viewers.

While an understanding that the franchise round was coming and that ATV (or at least ATV-as-it-was-then-structured) was unlikely to survive it, may have played a part in the end of the series, it does not seem to have been the only factor. Its stars fees made **Sapphire & Steel** an expensive programme to make[78], especially considering its place in the schedules, and despite its headline names, its

---

[76] *Counting Out Time*, 25m03s
[77] Chiefly books, such as P.J. Hammond's own novelisation of *Assignment One* and an Annual from Worlds Distributors.
[78] O'Riordan recalled, anecdotally, that McCallum's fee was £5,000 an episode. We should not necessarily take this off the cuff remark literally, but as producer this is information that O'Riordan was in a position to know and remember, and as a long-time friend of McCallum's he's unlikely to wildly caricature his finances on camera and on the record.

nature as a videotaped drama limited the possibilities for overseas sales[79].

David Collings has also suggested there was a 'general falling out'[80] around the time the serial was made, albeit one in which he himself was not involved, and that it was the cast and crew, rather than the broadcaster, who were keen to have the series end, and end memorably, at this point. 'The television company were very keen on the idea and they wanted to do another series, but then Joanna and David decided that they'd had enough of it by then, and didn't want to do anymore... I was very keen for it to go on.' Concurring with this, Hammond remembers having no great desire to continue writing the series[81] at this point. Perhaps it's the case that, given the situation, it would have required herculean effort for there to be more **Sapphire & Steel** for television at this point, and for a variety of reasons no one was either prepared, or in a position, to put that effort in.

Whatever the reasons for this being the last serial, it again seems that it was made rather quickly, despite little prospect of it being broadcast any time soon. The design plans for the serial[82] give VTR (i.e. Video Tape Recording) dates for the production as 20-23

---

[79] When it was marketed in the 1990s as one of the 'classics' of the ITC/ATV stable, and made available for repeats and on VHS, it was a notable exception as a multi camera videotape drama amongst a host of single camera film series.
[80] *Assigned* 72%. All participants in the final serial are, it must be said, enthusiastic about each other's contributions to the programme in *Counting Out Time*.
[81] *Counting Out Time*
[82] A (largely unclear) photograph of these is included as a PDF on Disc 6 of the 2007 Network DVD release of the whole series.

November 1980. While that might be thought to be only part of the serial's recording schedule, four studio days is about right for a hundred minutes of multi-camera VT drama c.1980. It is essentially the schedule that all twentieth century **Doctor Who**, the programme that **Sapphire & Steel** most resembles in many ways, was shot on, and is a schedule that would be considered sufficient for that amount of situation comedy material in the second decade of the 21st century. More importantly, the plan is for the entire studio set used for the serial.

Despite, or perhaps because of, this hurried schedule, David Collings has noted that the scripts for this serial were worked on extensively during rehearsals[83] and on set, with many of the changes instigated by star David McCallum, with the acquiescence of producer Shaun O'Riordan, to whom he was close. While modest about his own contributions McCallum, who even then had been a television star on both sides of the Atlantic for more than a decade, has a reputation for taking an interest in areas of production beyond simply his performance.

Hammond has been said not to have minded the way his scripts were treated by actor and producer[84], while Joanna Lumley has described this process, not unfondly, as 'boys' games'[85] she was reluctant to join in with and explained that she saw her role in the production as that of a performer, and what's more one playing a

---

[83] It must be said that it's not unusual for actors to over-rate the amount of rewriting done in rehearsals. Arguably, much of the rehearsal process is to allow actors to take ownership of a piece from its writer and the process can be deceptive to those within it.
[84] *Assigned 73%.*
[85] *Counting Out Time*, 8m50s

'maiden tied to the rock for the dragon'[86]. It's an interesting phrase that is perhaps more relevant to this serial than any other[87].

The extent of McCallum's contributions to the script are unlikely ever to be ascertained, but everyone agrees that one aspect of the serial was heavily modified at his suggestion during production. Hammond had written an ending which saw Sapphire, Silver and Steel trapped together for all eternity. McCallum objected on the grounds that the series was about its two leads. O'Riordan sided with McCallum, and Hammond folded. David Collings had concerns that this might be seen to imply that his character was in on the trap sprung on his colleagues but was persuaded otherwise.

Hammond's objection was in part because while he had written a cliffhanger ending for the series, with its leads (and in his conception of the scene, Silver also) seemingly trapped for eternity, he had also prepared a story 'out' that would allow the characters to escape from their prison, should more episodes of the series have been requested. However, this 'out' only works if Silver is among those trapped. He would have found cutlery made from the metal with which he shares his name, and with which he has a previously demonstrated affinity, and used it to create something to enable them to escape[88]. In the end, Central was not interested in continuing **Sapphire & Steel**, and McCallum's revision of Hammond's final cliffhanger became the end of the series, as well as the serial, as had perhaps always been likely to be the case. In later years Hammond would still insist that not having Silver in the

---

[86] *Counting Out Time*, 9m00s
[87] See Chapter Four.
[88] Commentary 6:4 10m20s

69

final scene was 'not something I would have wanted'[89] but later relented on reviewing the episode[90], conceding that 'McCallum was right' [91] McCallum, for his part, saw the ending as essentially sequel hunting, with the cliffhanger designed to provoke people into wanting to find out what happened to the characters, and thus make further episodes more, not less, likely.[92]

Too much television criticism is written as if the norms of American network television are universal[93], when they are not. While in American television drama, if not comedy, a definitive ending to a series is generally perceived to be a twenty-first century innovation, by 1980 it was already accepted practice that long running British television series tended to finish, rather than simply stop, presenting the audience with endings that made a statement about the programme as a whole.

Thus, George Bulman retires from the police[94] and Belgium is liberated from Nazi occupation[95]. Jack Ford is gunned down in

---

[89] *Counting Out Time* 26m00s

[90] It is clear from the conversation between O'Riordan and Hammond that their interviews for *Counting Out Time* were conducted earlier the same day as their joint episode commentaries.

[91] Commentary 6:4 24m4s

[92] *Counting Out Time* 25m26s

[93] I would argue that American and British television are not even the same medium. Or that they were not in 1980. There has been some convergence since.

[94] **Strangers**: *With These Gloves You Can Pass Through Mirrors* (20 October 1982)

[95] **Secret Army**: *Bridgehead* (8 December 1979) and *The Execution* (15 December 1979)

Spain[96], what remains of Blake's 7 are killed on the planet Gauda Prime[97] and Philip Martin's **Gangsters**[98] are destroyed in an explosion of metafictional flummery, to pick five prominent series that ended contemporaneously with **Sapphire & Steel**'s own run on television.

The ambiguity during production over whether the serial was definitively the ending or not, does not really matter. **Blake's 7** (1978-81), an almost exact contemporary of **Sapphire & Steel** and aimed at a similar audience[99], had an ending every year; a cliffhanger which could serve both as a final scene/conclusion for the series and a springboard to further episodes if it was required[100], and it's in this light, in the context of British television of the later 1970s and early 1980, that the finale of *Assignment Six* is best understood.

Curiously, while it is devastatingly brilliant, and exceptionally unlikely to be improved upon by any ill-advised revival, no matter how well-intentioned, the nature of **Sapphire & Steel**'s memorable ending is one of the few things about it which is demonstrably in no way unusual about it as a piece of television of its time.

---

[96] **When the Boat Comes In**: *Roll of Honour* (21 April 1981)

[97] **Blake's 7**: *Blake* (21 December 1981)

[98] **Gangsters**: *East of the Equator* (10 February 1976)

[99] David Collings appears in the final episodes of both.

[100] Although in practical terms by the time the last episodes of the first and second series were shot, **Blake's 7**'s production team knew they would be returning the following year. This was not the case, however, for the third series. A fourth series was ordered after the programmes had been produced and aired, because BBC executive Bill Cotton had been so impressed with the last episode of Series Three.

It was on Central, not ATV, on which the final **Sapphire & Steel** serial was broadcast, rattled through in around two weeks and, according to fan legend, billed as a repeat in the *TV Times* and newspaper listings due to a mistake made in sending out information about the programme. That could be seen as an ignoble end for a series launched with a *TV Times* cover, but the programme has had an afterlife denied to many ostensibly more successful television series. Released on VHS in 1992-93[101] and on DVD twice in this century, it has been repeatedly cited as an influence by television writers such as Mark Gatiss and Toby Whithouse, and like many television programmes with an active fan base, revived as a series of audio dramas by Big Finish productions.[102]

But for **Sapphire & Steel** as television, Tuesday 31st August 1982 was the end. Scheduled against as summer repeat of the hugely popular sitcom **Hi-De-Hi!** on BBC One and **Junior Pot Black**, a snooker competition for children, on BBC Two[103] it scraped a 15% viewing share against them[104].

---

[101] A release accompanied by a reprint of Hammond's novelisation of the first serial.

[102] Fifteen serials produced and released 2004-2008. None were written by Hammond or Read (Don Houghton died in 1991) and the only television cast member to return was David Collings. Mark Gatiss made several appearances as Gold, a character mentioned in the television series but who never appeared. The plays are, for rights reasons, no longer available except second hand.

[103] Channel 4 was not yet on air; it would not start broadcasting until 2nd November that year.

[104] Strangely appropriately, that night saw BBC One also show the final episode of its recent adaptation of *An Inspector Calls*, starring Bernard Hepton.

As recently as 2007 Lumley would express a desire to do 'one more episode!'[105] that would see the characters, played by the actors at their current ages, finally escape after decades, saying 'I didn't like us being up there. I still don't like us being up there'[106]

But up there they are.

2: 'Explain the Journey'

It is rare to think of television writers as having a 'canon'. That's not, in this case, 'canon' in the theology-derived sense beloved of fans of fictional worlds from Sherlock Holmes onwards, where decisions are made by writers, producers or fans as to what is 'real' or 'counts' towards the portrayal of that fictional world. It's the even more abstract idea of a writer having a defined set or body of work that can be examined in relation to itself: to be looked through for, for example, recurring themes, ideas or techniques[107].

Television writers who are generally regarded as being in possession of this semi-mythical object tend to be, like Dennis Potter, people who principally work in the areas of the single play (or later on single drama) or the self-created, self-penned limited series or serial. P.J. Hammond's work has almost entirely been in series and serial television, almost always in series created by other people, and written by, if not committee, then a huge number of

---

[105] *Counting Out Time*, 25m00s
[106] *Counting Out Time*, 25m 03s
[107] Such 'canons' do not tend be exhaustive. The canon of Charles Dickens was usually defined as his fourteen novels, with his books about children's history or travel writing excluded to the point where even enthusiasts for his fiction may not even be aware they exist.

73

freelancers. (E.g. **Z Cars**, for which Hammond wrote around thirty episodes, and which employed around a hundred different writers across its sixteen-year run.)

Sapphire & Steel is, of course, an exception to the general rule in Hammond's case; a series that he created and wrote most of, with the episodes he didn't write arising from circumstance rather than intent. It is, for the most part, undistilled Hammond. Not just his words and scenes, but his characters and his concept; a level of expression arguably only possible elsewhere in his career in his occasional single plays and standalone contributions to anthology series, rather than his episodes of Euston Films' series like **The Sweeney**[108] or **Special Branch**[109].

Hammond has said that his initial idea for **Sapphire & Steel**, then still called **The Time Menders**, was pitched to Thames Television Children's producer Pamela Lonsdale. He had worked with Lonsdale earlier in the decade on **Ace of Wands** and in 1978 wrote an episode of **Shadows**, the horror tinged children's anthology series she was producing. His episode *And for My Next Trick*, does not quite prefigure **Sapphire & Steel**, but it is not divorced from its concerns or tone, particularly those of *Assignment Two*.

The story concerns a children's party magician, Mr Devine, played by Clive Swift. While he lives in grubby lodgings and has an affinity with his landlady's daughter, Marion, who is in her early teens, Devine is not a remotely sinister figure. He's kindly, a little frustrated that his career has never taken of, and at sea in the

---

[108] *Pay Off*, 29 November 1976
[109] *Diversion*, 2 May 1974

world of the 1970s (an early scene has him being advised by the mother of a partygoer that his tricks should be more 'anarchic').

After one particular failed engagement, he discovers a batch of coloured eggs in his lodgings. They appear and disappear over several hours, before he accepts both that they are real, and that they can aid him by enabling to do incredible, inexplicable magic tricks. Despite Marion's realisation that every successful trick with the eggs causes a piece of Devine's own property to vanish from his room, Devine uses them in his act.

The episode's ending, in which Devine disappears in front of his audience, the final item 'claimed' by the eggs being the conjurer himself, can be read as tragic. We don't know where Devine has gone or what has happened to him, and he himself is the victim, rather than the performer, of the trick. But it can also be seen as celebratory, almost an apotheosis. This is the biggest cheer, the loudest ovation, he has ever got in his life. It is his moment of greatest success.

And for My Next Trick is a good example of Hammond as a distinctive writer, and how his contributions to other writers' or producers' series often seem at an odd angle to the parent programme, and often have more in common with his own other work than other episodes of the series of which they are part.

Hammond himself has argued that **Sapphire & Steel** juxtaposed the two kinds of television he had most often written; an 'investigative story combined with science fiction and pure fantasy'[110] *And for My Next Trick* is a good example of the latter. His work on the long-

---

[110] *Counting Out Time,* 5m50s

running **Z Cars** provides the former. His two-part **Z Cars** serial, *Breakage*[111] is instructive; a good example of both the benefits and the limits of looking at the serial television work of a writer in this way.

The serial has two parallel stories that do not particularly inform or connect with one another, except on a thematic level. In one, a building is 'haunted' by sobbing that seems to emanate from an empty roof area. In the other, a tramp who goes by the name 'George T Wood' (played by Fulton Mackay), initially makes a complaint that he has been robbed, but when the police are too busy to help him, finds that his unusual dress and lifestyle mean he's accused by other members of the constabulary of having something to hide, perhaps of having committed crimes himself.

Wood is an intriguing character, who speaks in an odd, elliptical manner, half anecdote and half fantasy, and could be seen as an inversion of, or a most positive take on, the same archetype as Johnny Jack. (We discover at the end that he 'collects names', and by the final scene has borrowed that of Geoffrey Whitehead's Detective Inspector and is using it to check into a new hostel. His ambition of returning to Scotland has clearly been disregarded now he has a new identity.)

Wood's itinerant, peripatetic nature, 'dropping out' after his national service ended decades before (Mackay was nearly fifty at the time of production) resonates with the plight of the unnamed sobbing, suited businessman whom we find is the source of the 'haunting' noises. By the end of the final episode, this nameless figure seems to have killed a PC by pushing him off the roof. In a

---

[111] 21-22 August 1972.

sense, there is a contrast between these two figures who have retreated from the modern world, one into a relatively harmless fantasy life where he is likely only to hurt himself, and another who has broken and, in the process, destroyed someone else.

Both figures are contrasted with the random, purposeless authoritarianism of Police Constable Bates, who arrested Woods despite the tramp being the complainant, after he refuses the PC's illegal demand that he empty his bag for him on the street. This presentation is of a thoroughly thick-eared policeman, who uses rules but does not feel bound by them, or even understand them, but who is comfortable in the society that neither 'Wood' nor the unnamed man in the suit can cope with. All of which feeds into the episode's conclusion of a long running subplot in that year's **Z Cars**, that of PC Joe Skinner being given a chance in the plainclothes Detective branch, only to discover that he didn't like the complexity of the job after all.

All these things combine to create something that manages to be 'about' living in the then modern world, but in a way that is influenced by concerns normally outside the scope of routine police drama. The episodes are directed in a very matter of fact way by Julia Smith[112], but the material could accommodate more of a fantastical visual style.

In Hammond's later **Z Cars** episode *Damage*, this is exactly what his writing receives. The opening scene, in which an incompetent

---

[112] Smith would later co-create **EastEnders** with then **Z Cars** script editor Tony Holland, and aside from her contributions to **Doctor Who** very early in her career, and her direction of the celebrated 1968 BBC **The Railway Children**, her work is almost always in overtly mimetic contemporary drama.

housebreaker attempts to access someone's home at night through a letterbox, only to have his hand trapped by a walking stick, then wrapped in string and set on fire, while his assailant makes no sound and he descends from threatening retribution to begging for mercy, is exactly as nightmarish as it sounds[113], thanks to Tina Wackerell's direction.

Notably, a scene later in the episode which includes regular characters that the original audience would have been well-disposed towards is shot in the same manner. The house's silent inhabitant clearly regards any approach to her front door at night as a threat, regardless of how the series usually asks us to regard the men at her door[114].

Wackerell also positions one of her cameras on the floor, or as close to it as makes no odds, during some scenes at the station. This has the effect of making a place familiar from most episodes of the series seem oppressive and disorienting, as it does to the recently arrested house burglar, who glories in the evocative name of Moon.

---

[113] Although the scene becomes blackly comic in retrospect when Moon reveals his childhood ambition was to be a postman. (He instead became a house breaker who uses letter boxes to gain access.)

[114] While a BBC staff director such as Smith or Wackerell would not have been able to choose the programmes they worked on, staff's preferences were often taken into account by producers, for the simple reason that having someone enthusiastic about the kind of programme you were trying to make often made for better television, in which context Wackerell's contributions to **Adam Adamant Lives!** (1966) and **Detective** (1968) are perhaps revealing of her interests.

Elsewhere in the episode, Hammond's writerly concerns impose themselves directly on the drama unfolding onscreen. What starts as an ironic, but sentimental, scene in which Sergeants Lynch and Stone discuss the life of a retired police officer ('Smooth hands and police tie, a lifetime of anecdotes to bore the young 'uns with') grows progressively darker until Slater mentions:

'A daft old sergeant, from this division, beer dribbling down his watch chain, trying to outdo all the others at creepy stories going on and on about how he found a dead baby's body in the woods twenty years go. Murdered? Stillborn? And the body was all done up with bits of string.'

It's an image as nightmarish as anything in **Sapphire & Steel**, and perhaps all the more so for merely being related, rather than seen. While the explanations for everything that happens in the episode turn out to be wholly literal, in a manner perhaps indebted to the 'supernatural explained' of early gothic novel writing, when faced with the domestic tragedy behind everything Stone is moved to demand that the secretive parents he is talking to 'come back to the real world... the one things happen in' and accept responsibility for their actions. (They have effectively had their daughter – the traumatised woman who attacked both burglar – under house arrest since adolescence, when she violated their strict religious principles.) Stone is motivated by a desire to see these people engage with life, rather than dwelling in a world of platitudes and abstracts, their response to everything being to invoke religious dogma or ostensible high mindedness, rather than deal with what is in front of them. Like George T Wood, they have retreated from a world they cannot cope with, and like the unnamed killer on the roof in *Breakage* but they have harmed others in the process.

79

A grace note in the story include another unnamed man who has left the lights and radio on all night in his house for years, following a break-in. He is as, though less obviously, traumatised as the shut-in daughter and the additional character helps bind the stories concerns together, making the piece a coherent whole. When, at the story's conclusion Stone espouses his theory that police work is merely to 'stand up to the bad 'uns and protect the not so bad 'uns,' he is articulating something not far from Sapphire and Steel's own credo, that there need to be those who protect the innocent, and even the not particularly innocent, when things happen to them that they did not bring upon themselves, and which violate a set of guiding principles.

At the same time that he was working on **Z Cars**, Hammond was effectively taking over creative responsibility for Thames Television's **Ace of Wands** from its creator, Trevor Preston, who was moving onto other things. While it is a mistake to talk of nineteen seventies serial television as having 'showrunners' in the modern, transatlantic sense, Hammond in a sense fulfilled this function on the third series of **Ace of Wands**. The first two series had been principally written by Preston, with other freelancers writing some serials (including Hammond, who wrote one for the second series). For the third series Hammond wrote ten out of the twenty episodes, including the opening serial, which introduced new regulars, and the final episode. He was effectively adopting Preston's own previous role.

Ace of Wands is the closest, of Hammond's own earlier works, to **Sapphire & Steel**. Tarot is a magician and is not formally charged with investigating supernatural crimes or preventing supernatural or alien incursions, but feels that his powers give him a certain responsibility in this regard. In all three series, Tarot has a female companion (Mikki in the final series, Lulli in the first two) with whom he has a psychic link, which can be used to warn of danger, generate cliffhangers and circumvent plotting issues, as in **Sapphire & Steel**. There is even an argument that the triangular relationship between Tarot, Lulli and Sam in the first two series resembles the later one between Sapphire, Silver and Steel, but with Steel and Silver's personalities largely swapped[115].

Ace of Wands is not as hard edged as **Sapphire & Steel**, and its moments of horror are less frequent. However, there are similarities in theme and tone. The mysterious Mr Peacock in Hammond's *Peacock Pie* has powers that enable him to distort people's perceptions of him and their surroundings that are not a million miles away from those of the Shape in *Assignment Four*. The story concludes with Peacock being trapped in his own mind. *The Meddlers* concerns itself with the consequences of digging into the ground in the process of redeveloping historic areas. *The Beautiful People* is about an alien incursion, and a trap disguised as a simpler kind of con trick, with an ending that leaves our heroes' future in doubt.

Hammond's work after **Sapphire & Steel** continues to investigate and work over the themes brought to the fore in his own series. Most overtly one of his episodes of 21st century **Doctor Who** spinoff **Torchwood** *From Out Of The Rain* concerns monstrous figures trapped in celluloid, and works as a riff on, and implicitly a direct sequel to, *Assignment Four*. Less directly, it is easy to see

---

[115] The first two series no longer exist, except for a handful of episodes extant as poor quality audio recordings, so this implication needs to be intuited from surviving scripts, rather than performance cues. There is no similar relationship in the surviving episodes, because Chas and Mikki are siblings.

themes that are foregrounded in **Sapphire & Steel** imposed on series that don't normally concern themselves with these areas. For example, one of Hammond's episodes of **Perfect Scoundrels**[116] concerns the digging up, for money, of a crashed WW2 plane that may, or may not, contain human remains. While there are no real suggestions of the supernatural, the piece is haunted in a less abstract sense. The realisation that the crashed plane is German, not Allied, and that the dead teenager at the controls, preserved in mud, is similarly not one of 'our boys' but 'the enemy' prompts lead Harry Cassidy to observe that it doesn't matter, as he is still 'some mother's son'.

Even with these few examples[117], the centrality of **Sapphire & Steel** to any Hammond canon is obvious; the series constitutes the most unadulterated version of Hammond's writing made for television. While *Assignment Two* is usually picked by fans as their favourite of the six serials, and Hammond himself vacillates between *Two* and *Four*, it is *Six* that constitutes the most unadulterated form of the series itself, the distillation of the distillation.

Sapphire & Steel are waiting for us at a 'nowhere sort of place', a 'waystation' at an indeterminate time between 1924 and now. It's time we joined them there.

---

[116] *Last of the Few*, 9 May 1992. The programme ran for three series, but Hammond only contributed to the third, which was made as one hour, rather than 30m, episodes and which tried to add depth and drama to a series that had initially concentrated on the 'comedy' side of its generic designation.

[117] I have generally chosen material which is available on commercial DVD, in order to make it easier for readers to follow up these programmes themselves if they wish.

3: Just Part of the Distraction'

In *Assignment Five* we saw 'It', as Sapphire and Steel termed their enemy, adopting an authorial mode. The programme's pastiche of genre conventions was in fact a conscious one indulged in by the serial's offscreen antagonist, who was playing at Agatha Christie. The mode of the story was, while often playful and certainly leavened with more humour than Hammond's own four earlier serials, interrogative. It was a series picking itself, and that which it had chosen to be a part of it, to pieces as part of its own dramaturgy.

This had not been an essential part of **Sapphire & Steel** before. While the first four serials have influences, the programme neither mocks nor interrogates them. Not only is it not arch, as *Assignment Five* is, it's also not deconstructive, which is its other strength. *Assignment Six*, consciously or unconsciously, adopts this aspect of *Assignment Five*. It is four episodes of a programme taking itself apart and examining itself both as a story and as an example of a visual storytelling medium.

In this context the long sweeping opening shot of the first episode, which clearly evokes and engages with the famous opening camera move of Orson Welles' *A Touch of Evil*, seems like an important statement. While Welles' film does not provide much else in terms of inspiration for the serial, like Welles' Vargas, Steel is a dogged, ambiguous investigator and both stories revolve around an investigation into matters surrounding a couple in love and their car.

The set for the garage is huge and impressive, and the camera movement around it is keen to show it off. That's understandable, but the shot goes on for so long, that it (perhaps?) inadvertently draws attention to the crisp cleanliness of the set, and thus its artificiality. For a moment, it looks so like a model it's a genuine surprise to see Sapphire watching forlornly out of the window. But then this is appropriate, because artificiality is something else that the serial is going to concern itself with.

Sapphire and Steel have recently arrived at the garage or 'service station' to find Silver already there. Steel has to have the concept of a garage explained to him and Sapphire settles for 'some kind of halfway place' when doing so. In the process she neatly encapsulates the settings for all of Hammond's own **Sapphire & Steel** serials and also prefigures this final one's end. Hammond has noted that he did not know how this serial was going to end when he began writing it[118] which makes it all the more remarkable that in hindsight and on second and subsequent viewings, everything about this serial seems inevitably heading towards it.

Sapphire also informs Steel that they are in 'the present'. This is in part a practical obfuscation; the production team had little idea when the serial would be transmitted, and in the end, it would be eighteen months after production that the serial was shown. It also facilitates the discussion of multiple time zones converging at the station that comes later, and allows for the introduction of the idea of the time loop the station is stuck in.

For while we are told 'there is no time' where the characters are, time clearly moves forward in practical terms. The characters are not, as they have been at earlier points in the series, frozen – either conscious or unconscious of the fact – and unable to act, converse

---

[118] Commentary 6:4 1m27s

84

and so on. But time itself, time as an abstract, is caught in a small loop, as the call to the speaking clock and switching on the radio demonstrate[119]. Silver himself has been there for six hours, but nothing around him has changed.

Silver was sent to anticipate the Time Break, but he says it had occurred before he arrived, although the couple arrived after him[120]. Sapphire understands and can establish that the 'real time' is around midnight, even though the station is 'stuck' at 8:54pm. Silver plays the station's state-of-the-art (for 1980) fruit machine, and cheats. 'Sometimes you're supposed to lose,' Sapphire chides him. 'Oh, I wondered why I wasn't enjoying it,' he replies. It's a nice warm moment between the two, part of the flirtation they enjoyed in *Assignment Three* and which is increased in this serial[121]. But again, it serves as a preview of the end of the serial.

The frequent flashes of the logo for Access, a prominent credit card in 1980, seem like a pun: how did they get here? It's the best use of the many contemporary product logos that litter the set, reinforcing the 'present' time frame. It also finds its opposite in the

---

[119] That the radio goes to a sports match of some kind where the looped moment is of 'the referee indicating' seems like a good grace note; when being explicitly directed by the referee the players are not in control of the game and cannot act to affect its outcome.

[120] Although later the Man will tell Steel that Silver arrived after they did. Is this a scripting mistake? Or is it an early indication that what the Man says is entirely invented for the agents' benefit?

[121] 'I'd love to,' he says as Sapphire touches his face, and at another point he kisses her palm. Neither Sapphire nor Silver respect each other's personal space, suggesting some sort of intimacy, emotional or physical.

moment where Steel uncovers an antiquated, but new, safety razor in the Man's car. Which surely cannot fail to remind of us of the scene in *Assignment Five* where the anachronism of a 1930s safety razor in 1980 was used as an indication of Mullrine's house becoming unstuck in time[122].

We return to the serial's interest in interrogating the programme of which it is a part when Silver reveals that the sound of the traffic behind the garage is looped, the same few moments of noise over and over again. While this leads into his demonstration that the garage is surrounded by a kind of time loop, this sort of looped sound is exactly how the background effect of traffic would have been achieved on television when needed, including in this production. It is almost as if the characters, like the actors who play them, are on a vast set in a studio, playing out a drama of which they're not the authors.

The other inhabitants of that set, that service station, a man and a woman (who are never named and only referred to as the Man and the Woman) have ostensibly arrived by accident, driving up to 'the present' from 1948. Silver has not asked them much during the six hours they have been sharing the garage as, as he tells Steel *'I'm not very good at intimidation'*, (i.e. Steel is, based on the previous serials). But this exchange exists to set up something odd and counterintuitive which happens almost immediately afterwards. Steel, perhaps at odds with his usual characterisation, is almost

---

[122] Steel also finds a newspaper, the *Sunday Despatch*, a real paper that ceased publication in 1961 when it was absorbed by the *Sunday Express*. Newspaper reports also play a role in the events of *Assignment Five*.

instantly worried about and concerned for the Woman, in a way that probably mimics the audience's initial response.

Edward De Souza's performance as the Man is detached, hard, yet laconic. He doesn't merely not ask for Sapphire and Steel's sympathy, for the audience's sympathy, he actively refuses it. Nothing he says is unreasonable, but he says it in a way that brooks no argument and invites no engagement. Johanna Kirby's Woman, on the other hand, is harried, panicked and desperate: 'It can't be a crime, can it?' she asks, unable to keep the despair out of her voice. She invites sympathy without asking for it, a subtle distinction from the Man, and thus presents as an Innocent.

The three Agents are suspicious of both the Man and the Woman until they tell them not to be. It's a classic confidence trickster's double bluff, relying on the assumption that a dishonest person would not raise the possibility of them being dishonest. 'This isn't a trick on our part you know,' says the Woman, 'It's not some sort of game.' Ultimately, that's exactly what it is; a trick, one being played by the Man and the Woman on Sapphire and Steel, and by the programme on its audience.

Steel's encounter with the Old Man in the 1928 version of the garage is nicely set up by this conversation, the Old Man having been introduced in conversation as a real person but also a local 'character'. Again, this flags up the artificiality of the situation. This is also something done by introducing the question as to why the lights of the station are on in the heights of summer. This is raised as if it is a matter of enormous importance to the assignment, but is within minutes answered prosaically by the Man. The Old Man who owns the garage in 1948 leaves them on at all hours[123]. Thus, things that 'should' be part of the investigation are revealed as individual human quirks; how a **Sapphire & Steel** story usually works is coming apart in front of us.

The recursive dialogue that has always featured in the series reaches new heights of deliberate absurdity and banality here, as The Man is asked how he knew the Old Man would be in and he replies 'Because he never goes out'. It's **Sapphire & Steel** at its most Pinteresque, simultaneously logical but meaningless; it also, yet again, points to where the leads will be at the end of Episode Four.

The couple, whom Sapphire immediately intuits are '...married, but not to each other,' (to Silver's visible surprise) also seem to reference *Assignment Five*. That was also a story about an adulterous affair between a much older man and a younger woman, and the consequences of that. As we'll discover, *Assignment Six* will also be such a story, but of a very different kind.

Hammond has repeatedly admitted that the plan when writing the first two episodes of this serial was *not* that Sapphire and Steel be trapped by this couple[124], this 'Man' and 'Woman' at least one of whom is a creature with powers like their own[125]. In light of this, it is worth asking what the plan, if any, was when these episodes

---

[123] The additional question as to why this would affect the lights of the 1980 garage is never answered — but then it is never asked.

[124] 'When I started episode one of this last story I didn't know that the people were going to be hunters, coming to catch [Sapphire and Steel].' Commentary 6:4 1m27s.

[125] 'Only half way through did it all make sense to me.' Commentary 6:4 1m40s.

were being written. What is the shadow version of *Assignment Six* that lies beneath its earliest episodes? What ending are they pointing to, if any?

'Where were you going when you drove in here for petrol? There are suitcases in your car,' says Steel at the Episode One/Two cliffhanger/reprise. This revelation that he has searched their car prompts the first strong, emotional response from the Man and the Woman. The Man leaps to his feet as Steel mentions 'consequences' and seems prepared to strike him when he says 'It's obvious you're both running away from something'. A little earlier, the Woman insists 'We don't have to,' as Steel suggests she answer his questions, perhaps invoking the absolute 'right to silence' arrested suspects then had in UK criminal law.

This is an interpretation shored up by the following scene, when the Man, calmer now, informs Silver that he and the Woman are lovers, 'running away' from their respective spouses: '*That's* not exactly an arrestable offence now, is it?' he says, and Edward De Souza's emphasis seems quite careful. *That's* not an *arrestable* offence, adultery being a tort, i.e. the civil law equivalent of a crime, but it is a serious matter of civil law. But then the Man says 'Adultery, they can't hang you for it'. What they could hang you for in 1948, however, was murder.

The Woman's determination not to give Steel their names, not even to use the Man's name when talking about or to him, would fit with them needing to keep their identities secret. Her fear of the Man going outside would fit with a desire not to be seen, as would the ways her eyes constantly flick to the main window during conversation[126]. The Man is very keen for Silver not to have access to the suitcases in the car's boot. What might the aforementioned razor, introduced in close up a few minutes before, have been used for?[127]

One plausible extrapolation of these moments, one which fits neatly with Sapphire sensing 'violence… from the past' and the Woman's panicked worries about whether something is or is not a crime, is that the couple are fugitive killers of some kind. A sort of provincial British Bonnie and Clyde[128] who have found themselves unstuck in time. Perhaps they have murdered their own spouses before running away together.[129] Perhaps, for reasons the story never quite gets round to implementing, they have murdered the Old Man?[130] This would fit very neatly with Sapphire's comments in Episode One concerning 'fear and violence' and 'a powerful emotion from the past'.

The trio of agents second meeting with the Old Man, near the end of Episode Two, also fits neatly with this interpretation. The Old Man is increasingly panicked as Sapphire, Silver and Steel come into view, asking 'Are you wanting service? Only that's at the front of

---

[126] The final episode will, yes, provide a different explanation for these elements, but that is beside the point.

[127] This might link to Silver's insistence in Episode Three that objects retain 'memory' of that for which they are used?

[128] Bonnie Parker (1910-1934) and Clyde Barrow (1909-1934) were infamous robbers and murderers who engaged on a crime spree in Depression era America before being killed by police in an ambush.

[129] I am indebted to Gareth Roberts for contributing this suggestion, and for discussions that allowed it to progress further.

[130] 'That image we saw earlier, the old man. Perhaps it was something to do with him?' says Silver shortly afterwards.

the building, not here. This is private here. This is private, this part of the building. Private property. You shouldn't be here.' Sapphire, as usual, is the one to note human emotion: 'Why are you frightened of us?' she asks.

This material is somewhat lost onscreen, despite appearing twice in the story as viewed, because the cliffhanger itself concerns the time jump. Hammond's admission that the story was largely written without knowing that the ending that appeared on screen would be the ending does not mean there was no rewriting done once that ending had been reached. The essentially irrelevant nature of the way time shifts forward at key moments during the story, including the Episode One cliffhanger, is ultimately explicable as 'just part of the distraction', but could also be conjectured as an imposition on the script, a quick addition or rewrite, in order to shift the emphasis away from the mystery of the couple and what they are doing or have done.

Watched in isolation, ignoring the ending we know is coming, the mystery of the couple is a key part of the second episode particularly; it's exceptionally substantial for a 'red herring'[131]. As with the material concerning the real lives of the Mullrine clique in *Assignment Five*, it doesn't really matter whether the details here are simple distraction within the fiction, or internal evidence of paths unfollowed by the real life writer(s); because although Hammond's admission that there *was* an unfollowed path in this instance makes some speculation irresistible, that in both stories there is an author within the fiction as well as one outwith it,

---

[131] Need it be said, this seems like another derivation from *Assignment Five* and its adoption of a Golden Age crime novel mode of storytelling.

inevitably makes matters like this even more unclear than they would otherwise be.

It is also at this point in Episode Two that the idea of the story being 'a trap' is first mooted. While Steel panics and worries, Sapphire asks him a series of questions that indicate that she is already beginning to work out what is happening to them, 'Supposing "It" is waiting for *us*?' she suggests to a not particularly comprehending Steel. 'Why Silver? Why is he here?' she also asks. Perhaps that question is answered shortly afterwards when the Specialist offers his opinion that 'My first thought is everything is haphazard, a mess. Time just jumbled up together, making no sort of sense... my second thought is that everything is too haphazard. It's too obvious. It's like something that's been *designed*.'

What is yet more interesting is that Silver is looking at Sapphire as he says it, as if he knows that she is more likely to grasp what he's suggesting than Steel is. It's one of numerous small hints in the story that Silver and Sapphire's rapport goes beyond mere flirtation; earlier in this episode they have shared a glance as Steel has critically observed of the Man and the Woman, that they are a 'loving couple... they are only human, aren't they?' The way they look at each other suggests they understand something that Steel doesn't. Which is not to say that Silver and Sapphire should be construed as lovers, simply that they have an insight into human feelings that Steel lacks.

It's at this point that time again moves forward seemingly arbitrarily, as it did near the end of Episode One, shifting by twenty minutes, so that it is now raining outside. But here it does so as Silver gets too close to the truth of what he and his colleagues are up against, as he decides that they can and should attempt to leave the service station. The jump forward distracts him from this intention, as does the almost immediate additional oddity of the rain stopping without time changing again, something that should be impossible given the Agents' own understanding of time and how it works.

Hammond is here explicitly unpicking the logic of his own story, his own programme, his own *sort* of story, in a manner which resembles the way Read and Houghton (at least attempted to) unpick Agatha Christie. Over the remaining half of the story, more threads will be unpicked, but first we have the arrival of a new character into this strange environment, a distraction for both the audience and characters who have got rather to near the truth.

4: 'Got a kiss for Johnny Jack?'

Johnny Jack is instantly a disruptive presence in the world of the story, distracting Silver and Sapphire from their line of thought about the overly designed nature of the plot in which they are engaged, but also churning up the relationships established amongst the service station's odd collection of inhabitants over the previous hour. In particular, his leering, even threatening[132], attentions paid to both Sapphire and the Woman are unsettling for the audience as well as the characters[133].

---

[132] The Woman refuses to be left alone with him, leading the Man to ask what Jack has done. 'Nothing, it's what he might do.' she replies, shivering.
[133] Sapphire is effective in pretending to be charmed by him, treating Johnny how he likes, even expects, to be treated, in order to get information from him. This is both an effective demonstration of how threatening circumstances can force women to behave, but also one of the serial's examples of turning a threat back on its originator.

It's also demonstrative of the way this story offers the first real intrusion of sexuality and adult romantic or sexual attachment into the series as written by Hammond. Previously, such things had not really been part of **Sapphire & Steel**. That's not just because of the strange, if refreshing, manner in which a series with two lead characters played by actors regarded as sex symbols by huge sections of the audience completely avoids hinting at a romantic attachment, or unresolved sexual tension between the two characters; it's also true of the situations in which they find themselves, and the guest characters they encounter.

Assignment One concentrates on children. *Assignment Two* has only a single 'real' other character, an old man without anyone else to talk to. The couple in *Assignment Three* though specifically 'a couple' do not act in a romantic manner at any point, and everyone in *Assignment Four* is very much alone. Again, this is an example of Hammond drawing on the work of the other people to write **Sapphire & Steel**; it is *Assignment Five* that introduces the idea of **Sapphire & Steel** stories having plot or character elements motivated by human sexuality.

What is particularly interesting about this intrusion is the way it links to the possibility of Johnny Jack being seen as a kind of mirror or inversion of Silver. Jack has Silver's mercurial, but happy go lucky, demeanour. (He isn't bothered by the idea of being in the future, nor terrified like the Woman and the Man.) Like Silver, and no one else in the story, Johnny Jack has longish curly hair, and wears a grey suit with an ostentatious, but still grey, waistcoat; the production is inviting us to look at the two characters in relation to each other.

In this context, Jack's leering could be seen as a crude simplification of Silver's flirtation, a contrast with both that and Steel's sexlessness[134]. His intrusion into the relationship of the Man and the Woman, while unwelcome, is not unlike Silver's imposition on Sapphire and Steel themselves. We have already seen, and it will later be made apparent again, that Steel does not entirely trust Silver, and it seems that this stems from the way the third agent disrupts Sapphire and Steel's partnership. It is not that Steel is jealous of the *way* that Silver interacts with Sapphire – he still seems to have no feelings of that kind at all – it's that he's jealous that someone else interacts with Sapphire at all – as in the aforementioned moment when he seems unsure how to relate to the Man and the Woman as a couple, to Silver and Sapphire's mutual recognition. This odd note will become increasingly important as this final serial moves to its end.

If Johnny is a version of Silver, then it follows that logically the Man and the Woman are meant to parallel Sapphire and Steel themselves. Once the thought occurs it becomes rather obvious; the Man is taciturn, contemptuous, brusque. He is prone to sudden violence, and then ameliorating it through conversation, but not apology. Comparisons between the Woman and Sapphire are harder, but for all but one scene of the serial the Woman is playing a part, affecting to be downtrodden, scared and on the run, rather than — as we shall see — the mastermind behind everything. But even in her roleplaying, there are some parallels. She usually understands what is happening more quickly than the Man does, just as Sapphire usually sees through things before Steel. There is also the nature of the role she adopts, not so far from 'the maiden

---

[134] Johnny's boasts of his 'family' and the 'Children on his back' seem to constitute a frequent boast of virility and are of a piece with his leering.

tied to the rock for the dragon,' as which Joanna Lumley has often described her own character.

Perhaps most importantly, as Sapphire glimpses the future at the climax of Episode Three she sees Steel and herself as black shadowed cut outs, just as she and the audience have already seen the Man and the Woman. This surely invites us to seek parallels between the two pairs? And how does she describe those who have come to hunt them down: 'like us, almost exactly like us'. She is not referring solely to the nature of their powers.

Johnny Jack has plot and story functions as well as having thematic points to make, of course. His conversation about his trade also seems to point to the eventual resolution of almost all plot elements of this serial as existing merely there to distract our leads. He says he's from a company, prompting Sapphire to ask 'A company of performers? And you're one of them?' He confirms this, and then suggests that he might 'put on a bit of a show later'. Which, of course, in concert with the Old Man, the Man and the Woman, he will. His comments about waiting at the station for the rest of his company also further align him with Silver (who had to wait six hours for Sapphire and Steel to arrive) and again points at the way the trap is waiting to be sprung[135].

Because, whatever he says, Johnny is, as all second time viewers of the serial know, another mere distraction. But it's worth returning to the question of what he may represent for the lost version of the

---

[135] Christopher Fairbank's superb performance showcases some of Hammond's most threateningly abstract, elliptical dialogue ('Where did I come from? How can I answer that?' 'You forget?' 'I don't have to remember'.)

story where the service station mystery is not a deliberate trap. It is easy to imagine a version of the story where the threatening but ultimately weak Johnny Jack — Steel easily bests him physically — is the victim of a more domestic, middle class sort of murder, one committed by the Man and the Woman. Perhaps more plausibly, he could, given the second episode's emphasis on capital punishment, be someone hanged for the murder of the Old Man committed by the Man and the Woman. While most murders are committed by people known to the victim, blaming a murder on an unknown passer-by or peripheral figure is a common, if desperate, strategy by those who have killed someone they know.

Who would the world of twentieth century Britain be more likely to believe was responsible for the killing of an old man: a respectable couple in a nice new car, or a leering tambourine player in a mucky jacket? (It might be conjectured that this is why, uniquely amongst the station's inhabitants, he has a name. If the resentment and violence felt by Sapphire in Episode One is at the injustice meted out to Jack, the other figures in the story are people he never really knew.)

The itinerant man is a figure who turns up periodically in Hammond's work, and Johnny Jack represents that figure in its most fascinating form, which is all the more remarkable given how little the character actually features, what with his not arriving until Episode Three, and his being transformed into the clean shaven, suited version of himself at the end of the same episode.

As part of how it sets up parallels between most of its characters, the latter section of this story also asks us to look at Silver in relation to Steel. In Episode Three we see Steel trying and failing to play the fruit machine that Silver had so easily conquered earlier, as if he is reaching towards trying to be more like Silver. Almost at the end of Episode Three they have an extraordinary conversation, prompted by Silver's theft of Johnny Jack's tambourine, that serves as an extended metaphor for their different approaches, which is worth quoting (almost) in full.

SILVER

If it's a musical instrument, it's never been played. Every musical instrument that ever was or is, is its own recording device, did you know that?

STEEL

No.

SILVER

That's just a noise. It's as if this instrument has only ever made a noise, never music.

STEEL

Well, it's a drum, isn't it? You can't expect it to make a tune.

SILVER

No, but we can expect it to make music. Its own sort of music.

It's almost an argument between poetry and prose, as well a discussion of the two men's methods of investigation. Steel the literalist, Silver drawn to abstractions that provide a way through. This seems important given that Silver has already worked out what is going on but has been pushed away from considering its implications by his colleagues, particularly Steel, and the continuing nature of the distractions supplied by the service station.

There is one more, big distraction to come. When the Woman seems to break away from the Man and decides to tell the agents 'what is going on' she insists that she will only talk to Steel. In doing so, she appeals to his humanity, but also to his vanity. She won't talk to Sapphire, because she knows Sapphire will see through her. And because she knows that it's an effective way of driving, however, briefly, a wedge between the two, which will limit their effectiveness, limit their possibilities for escape.

The Old Man, the Man and Johnny Jack transform into their suited and booted selves when Silver reaches, and tries to disable, the barrier around the service station. All the way through this serial the implication has been that everyone is waiting for something, some kind of event. Yes, this is the springing of the trap, but while it is not made as clear as it could be, it seems that that springing is brought forward because of Silver's almost successful action. Which would justify the further attempts to distract him in particular since his successful intuiting of the actual problem, if not the plan, at the end of Episode Two.

Now, though, Sapphire has a vision, prompted by the Woman. She is genuinely shocked, even distraught as she tells Steel what she now understands. Steel dismisses this as a trick on Sapphire she hasn't seen through, but again she's right and again he's wrong. 'I was sensing violence. Our destruction, yours and mine,' she says.

By the end of the Episode Three Hammond has, in effect, unmade his own programme entirely. Undone it. Over the previous seventy-five minutes, clues have turned out not to be clues. Victims have turned out to be perpetrators[136]. Eccentric characters have turned out to be affectations. Questions have been discovered to be deliberately unanswerable, not merely unanswered. And the relationship between the programme's central characters has been parodied, and then shaken.

The final episode is very different to any episode of **Sapphire & Steel** before it, as the series' leads are hunted and finally defeated by an enemy 'almost exactly like us', but even before the final trap is sprung on them, Sapphire and Steel have been, in effect, stuck in a **Sapphire & Steel** story, one authored by their enemies rather than (or rather, *as well as*) P.J. Hammond, and unlike the time their enemy stuck them into an Agatha Christie pastiche, this time there can be no escape.

5: 'Forever'

According to P.J. Hammond, the opening scene of the final episode of **Sapphire & Steel** was written at the request of the actors who played them, in order to clarify and quantify some of their motivations[137]. While it couldn't be said to do exactly that, it does perhaps give us more detail about Sapphire and Steel's world than the rest of the series put together.

---

[136] The second episode of the first serial had established, again perhaps paradoxically, that the 'time' is both the corridor surrounding all things that, when it becomes thin and damaged allows humans to be threatened by paradoxes, and *also* that 'time' is that which breaks through endangering humans when said corridor becomes thin. That the characters who present as the story's victims are revealed to be its antagonists is an interesting echo of this.

[137] Commentary 6:4

Sapphire has already compared their opponents to themselves, and after the opening titles this is followed up. Steel says that 'they' asked him to work for them once, and that he chose not to. This is followed by Sapphire confirming that she too was asked and also declined. This is immediately after Sapphire's explanation that 'they answer to a higher authority', although it is not explicit if 'they' is being used to refer to one, or two, groups of people across the conversation. 'They' here (which serves a similar function to 'It' in *Assignment Five*) seems to mean the superiors of the Man, the Old Man and Johnny Jack, whereas in the cliffhanger to Episode Three, it seemed to mean the men themselves.

This elision, which isn't atypical of Hammond's writing, allows the scene to obscure as it reveals. Was it their hunter's superiors, that 'higher authority', who independently asked both Sapphire and Steel to join them? Or was it the 'hunters' (as Hammond calls them on the commentary track on the last episode) themselves. How personal is this attack on the agents? 'They resent us... They resent our achievements,' says Steel angrily, and Sapphire suggests that it is their 'independence' that is resented. Both agree that this independence, that led them both to reject overtures from 'they' not knowing the other had or would do the same, is why they 'work so well together'.

That 'work' seems to be important: Steel refers to what he and Sapphire do as 'a job' in *Assignment One*, and in *Assignment Five* we discover that their powers can be gifted to ordinary humans, and that they come in 'levels'. We might intuit from this that Sapphire and Steel are, or were, human, but Steel's dismissive comment about how sending us 'here' at the start of this story could also be read as referring to the Earth[138]. This conversation, and McCallum is extraordinary throughout it, is arguably the first time Steel looks scared in the whole series. He looks weary. He seems to be having an actual human emotion for the first time and Steel's new emotionality is important to the frantic, helter-skelter pace of the first 18 minutes of the last episode.

So that's Sapphire and Steel. What about their enemies? Their 'hunters'? This discussion contains implications of a hierarchical structure, with the Transient Beings/hunters (or their employers) above Sapphire and Steel (or *their* employers). But it also suggests that the relationship between the two groups is like the then contemporary Cold War between East and West. Perhaps, though, it is more like the occasional conflicts between civilian police and domestic security services that have been known to arise, e.g. between Special Branch and MI5 in the UK.

There is certainly a sense of Steel being familiar with these other parties in something more than the abstract as he spits out 'They always were better organised!' When Steel later discusses their opponents with Silver, he reflects 'what better choice?' could there be of someone to bring them down. But when Silver suggests the involvement of Transient Beings, Steel is unconvinced. 'The Transient Beings are locked in the past, where they belong,' he says. It's another brilliant piece of casual world-building. Two people familiar with a thing can talk about it without expressing it fully, by only alluding to shared knowledge, like a sort of reverse info-dump. 'They can change shape and move anywhere, but only the past. They cannot move forward in time,' insists Steel. Here we

---

[138] Given Lumley's belief that Sapphire and Steel were aliens, do they have other Assignments fixing time on other planets? How do they appear there?

see that Silver is more flexible than Steel, able to contemplate changing rules, or that the information that he has is out of date, both things with which Steel struggles.

It is never absolutely confirmed that these hunters are 'Transient Beings', but the Agents proceed on the assumption that they are, and the conversation which follows about being trapped in the past, and the 'hunters' need for a machine would seem to indicate that they are. On the DVD commentary for this episode, Hammond briefly conflates the Transuranic Heavy Elements of the opening titles and the Transient Beings of this story when talking to O'Riordan[139], something that fan responses to the series have also often done. It may be that they were intended to be one and the same, and that the similarity of the names was not a coincidence, as well as them both being the hunters of this story. Other views are available.

Later, when the Man and Johnny Jack are interrupted in their attempt to execute Silver using a time shift, we see that they are not responsible for the movement forward in time that has been dogging the characters throughout the story. Silver theorises that Time itself is fighting back against the damage being done to it but would that seem to make the occasions when time shifts at the moments which are absolutely convenient for the Man's objectives too much of a coincidence to be countenanced. What's important is that the time shift enables Silver to escape. Is this an imposition by the serial's real-world author, P.J. Hammond, or the author of the trap itself?

---

[139] Commentary 1:1 5m5s

A fine grace note here is that there are three different buildings, and three different time periods, which finds some reflection in the sending of the hunters back to the Triassic[140], but also in the trio of Sapphire, Silver and Steel. Whatever they ultimately are, the Old Man and Johnny Jack, while threatening presences, are easily dispatched to the Triassic by Silver and Steel, and even before then take a back seat to the Man and the Woman, whose relationship with each other and disputable nature come into focus in this last few minutes, before and leading into the episode, the serial and the series' final scene.

Earlier in the story Steel has spoken contemptuously of the Man and Woman as a 'loving couple' and has tried to understand love by expressing it to the Woman as her being able 'to forgive him almost anything,' something which the Woman then denies. (There is a beautiful moment of confusion in Steel's face as she says 'I love him' of her unnamed partner.) Here, he grabs the woman roughly, demanding that she tell him everything about the Man's objectives, despite her already having offered to do so. When she does tell him, it makes for grim hearing: 'He's been sent here to kill you, simple as that.'[141]

How much of what she says can we as an audience trust? Someone viewing this episode for a second or subsequent time knows that the Woman is not just part of the plan, she is in on it, she is one of its creators. Sapphire and Silver question the Woman's unconvincing change of heart, and her bland explanation that all she wants is for no one to get hurt.

---

[140] The term refers literally to 'three kinds' of rock.
[141] And a few moments later '...to trap you, to trick you'

Why should she help us? Why is she telling us all this?

And later

What sort of trick are you playing?'

The revelation that the woman has some sort of machinery built into her, and her subsequent collapse, changes Steel's attitude entirely. He comes to see her as a victim, as he and Sapphire and Silver are now victims, of the machinations of the Transient Beings. He becomes desperately concerned for the well-being of a woman who, minutes previously, he was interrogating. He explains that they have a responsibility to her. It is as if, with no victory possible, and with survival the only objective, Steel has become concerned at last with protecting the innocent. Sapphire is given the job of helping the woman to the barrier, Silver and Steel will follow. Steel is not, here, the man who sacrificed Tully to appease an army of angry ghosts. It could be said that it is Steel's rarely expressed, perhaps newly emerging, humanity that kills them, but Steel's failure to understand the relationship between the Man and the Woman is just as important, and the story has one more trick up its sleeve, in its luxuriously long final scene.

As Sapphire and Steel arrive in the diner in the final scene, they face a strange inversion of their arrival from the first episode. Some dialogue is repeated or repurposed, but this time it is Steel who is hesitant and afraid. The Woman is now dressed as if for a funeral, but she looks happy for the first time in the serial. Soon we'll understand why. Steel is still preoccupied with saving her. Pushing her behind him as he threatens the Man with the Chess Box device, he is astounded to realise that she is, at least, an equal partner in whatever it is that the Man has planned and executed at this 'in between sort of place'. Steel still cannot conceive of her as having, despite his own status, agency.

The Woman tells The Man 'We did it'. He then stares lovingly at her as she explains the plot and delivers the episode's dramatic punchline. It's a reference back to her 'Romantic, isn't it?' comment at the top of the episode, when she tells Steel mid-interrogation that 'he chose me'. There can be no doubt they are equal partners in whatever enterprise it is that has brought them there, something that flatly contradicts Silver's initial Episode One instinct that the Man does not let the Woman speak for herself. More, it's an inversion of the cliché of women in fiction as the trap, and as bait, and as the victim.

P.J. Hammond has commented that when writing most of the serial he had 'no idea the woman was in on it' and if Steel's assumptions reflect the writer's, this is an even more brilliant piece of improvisation on the latter's part. 'This is the trap,' she says, and she is not merely drawing attention to what the trap is, she is pointing out what the trap is not.

It is not her. She is not a victim. She is not bait. She does not need rescuing. She is their enemy. The Woman and the Man, so often presented as a kind of dark mirror of Sapphire and Steel now seem lighter than them. Luxuriating in each other's company. Whatever they have done, it is clear they have done it for each other, and for the love they share. They are suddenly warmer than our heroes. They smile lovingly at each other. And then they are gone.

Sapphire seems to explain to Steel that she expected this, but he doesn't notice. And it's here that the story has its final twist. Earlier in the episode, we see the Old Man offer Silver a deal, saying that it is Sapphire and Steel's 'time' but not necessarily his. We also see that Steel, quite unfairly, doesn't quite trust Silver[142], who clearly has no thought of betraying his colleagues[143], and then is quick to use the Old Man's machine against him.

When Sapphire earlier encounters the Man at the edge of the barrier, she is alone. She is carrying the near comatose woman, and Silver and Steel are still back in the cafe. He mocks her, and asks her why she is trying to escape, when she knows it isn't possible. She has seen the future. Sapphire summons Steel and Silver to where she is, telepathically. But when they arrive, she says nothing. Sapphire seems frozen, immobile — she is no longer holding the woman as she was in the previous shot. Still she doesn't move. Still she doesn't say anything either as her colleagues arrive, or as they are threatened by the Man, or as Steel desperately tries to open his box first, or as Silver pointedly steps out of the frame and is never seen again. What has changed while the audience's attention has been elsewhere?

If the Old Man can offer Silver a deal, surely the Man is in a position to offer deals to other members of the party? The Man is a creature capable of love, and is in love, as we have seen and will see again. What might he understand about what people are prepared to do for each other? What sort of deal might he be able

---

[142] Their bad-tempered exchange, Silver: 'I'll tell you on the way', Steel: 'No, you'll tell me now!' seems particularly telling.
[143] David Collings was concerned that this might be seen as an implication during production, but this is not the same as taking it as a reading of the final serial.

107

to offer, and to whom? This is something interesting that has been lost by fixating on the question of whether Silver is in on the trap. (When he clearly isn't[144].) Sapphire has already seen the future, telling Silver as she does so that 'Hours will become days and months, and years will become thousands of years,' and she has already told Steel that she has sensed 'Our destruction, yours and mine... *our* future.'

She reprises that statement in the series' final moments: 'I saw the future, and it was our future.'

Their future.

But not Silver's. Has Sapphire, knowing she and Steel cannot escape, sacrificed both of them for Silver? Has the Man saved Silver from his colleagues with a time shift already, knowing that he can offer his freedom to Sapphire? Is this what she is trying to tell Steel as she insists 'I saw the future, and it was *our* future'?

Silver is, of course, the biblical reward for betrayal. Is Silver's life Sapphire's reward for betrayal?

In the final shot, Sapphire and Steel are staring directly towards the camera, out of a window that hangs in the sky, in the starfield in which they are trapped. They stare at us and we stare directly back at them; they are doubly trapped, in the frame of the television

---

[144] Fan worries over this idea may have their origins in a combination of this, that (in the first shot of this episode) the transformation of the Transient Beings seems to be triggered by something Silver does at the barrier, which could be interpreted as either a signal or an attempt to escape, and the very odd way Silver steps out of frame in the penultimate scene.

screen as well as in the window it contains. The Woman may as well have be addressing the audience directly as she said 'This is the trap, and it's nowhere, and it's forever.'

And here we are still.

Bibliography

Books

Callaghan, Richard, *Assigned! The Unofficial and Unauthorised Guide to Sapphire & Steel*. Prestatyn, Telos Publishing (2010). ISBN 9781845830328.

Christie, Agatha, *The Mirror Crack'd from Side to Side*. New York, Doubleday Dell (1962). ISBN 9780553350159.

Film

Hamilton, Guy, dir, *The Mirror Crack'd*. Associated Film Distribution (1980).

Plays

Priestley, J.B., *Time and The Conways* (1937).

Priestley, J.B., *An Inspector Calls* (1945).

Television

Ace of Wands. Thames, 1970-72.
       Peacock Pie.
       The Meddlers.
       The Beautiful People.

Web

'2nd Test, West Indies tour of England at London, Jun 19-24 1980',
http://www.espncricinfo.com/series/17053/scorecard/63267/engl
and-vs-west-indies-2nd-test-west-indies-tour-of-england-1980/

England v Australia 1930',
http://www.espncricinfo.com/wisdenalmanack/content/story/151
745.html

'Silver Jubilee',
http://www.kaldorcity.com/people/dcinterview.html

Biography

James Cooray Smith is a freelance writer and critic whose credits include *The New Statesman*, *Prospect*, *Private Eye*, *Hero Collector* and *That Mitchell and Webb Sound*. He researched and wrote the production information subtitles for several official BBC **Doctor Who** DVD releases and is the author of the well-received *The Black Archive #2: The Massacre* and *The Black Archive #14: The Ultimate Foe*.

He lives in North London with a Lady Barrister and their son, and can be found on twitter, usually talking about **Doctor Who**, as @thejimsmith.

Acknowledgments

Thanks to Sonja Adjin (@BARB) Ralf Collie, Saliya Cooray, Stuart Douglas, Toby Longworth, Gareth Roberts and Eddie Robson for, in varying combinations, useful bits of knowledge, research help, ideas I've pinched, sounding board services and going along with my flights of fantasy.